THE WELSH OF TENNESSEE

To

KEN NILSEN,

a fluent speaker of four Celtic Languages,

and whose encouragement led to my continued interest

in one such language.

THE WELSH OF TENNESSEE

Eirug Davies

Cover photograph: McCrary and Branson
Cover design: Y Lolfa

ISBN: 978 1 84771 429 9

FSC

Published and printed in Wales
on paper from well managed forests
Y Lolfa Cyf., Talybont, Ceredigion SY24 5HE
e-mail ylolfa@ylolfa.com
website www.ylolfa.com
tel 01970 832 304
fax 832 782

Contents

Figures

Introduction

OVER 300 WELSH-LANGUAGE BOOKS and pamphlets were published in the United States during the 19th century and close to half of those are included in the Celtic book collection of Harvard University's Widener Library. Readily apparent in many of them are the names of their former owners, from the Ap madog who contributed so much to the country's *eisteddfod* cultural festivals, to Robert Everett, who, in 1840 started his long association with the highly successful monthly magazine, *Y Cenhadwr Americanaidd* [The American Missionary]. As prominent as many such previous owners were, hardly anything is known of the individual whose name appears most frequently. To make his identity more intriguing still is the fact that he did not reside in the more northern part of the country as his Welsh contemporaries invariably did. This individual who was recognized for contributing the books to Harvard was a David R Thomas from Coal Creek, Tennessee. However, as one of the authors had noted within the book, his intention was to present it as a "small token of friendship" to a Rees R Thomas; there is some doubt as to whether David R Thomas was indeed the collection's original owner.

Coal Creek was one of several mining communities in Tennessee and the border area of Kentucky which came into being shortly after the Civil War. Behind such endeavours were some of the more enterprising Welsh who had previously been employed in the industrialized regions of Pennsylvania and Ohio. As to Coal Creek itself, it is located about 30 miles north-west of Knoxville but, by 1936, the name would be gone and Lake City favoured instead. This change reflected the presence of a nearby lake which resulted from a dam being built across the Clinch River by the Tennessee Valley Authority. Four miles away and closely associated with Coal Creek was Briceville, and towards the end of the 19th century both places came under national scrutiny when the miners defied state authority and rebelled against the use of convict labour in the mines. Other mining communities were to follow, and many of the key positions within the iron industry, both in Knoxville and Chattanooga, were also occupied by experienced Welsh workers.

Yet despite the accomplishments of those in the aforementioned places, about the only Welsh whose presence in Tennessee has been widely recognized in Wales itself, are those who arrived just prior to the Civil War, under the leadership of a Rev. Samuel Roberts. Having preceded them (or arrived shortly afterwards) were a few others of Welsh descent, and whilst they all merit some attention, of main concern here is learning more about the likes of Rees and David Thomas of Coal Creek, who went on to contribute so much to the early industrial development of Tennessee.

Amongst those who have been particularly helpful during this study are Bailey Francis, a descendant of a Dowlais, Kentucky family, John Kesterson MD, a descendant of a Coal Creek family, Billy McNamara, a descendant of one of the few Knoxville Welsh families who had remained loyal to the Anglican Church, J D Bailey and Edith Bradley Dickey, brother and sister and great-grandchildren of the David Richards and Iorthyn Gwynedd who were once so influential amongst Knoxville's Welsh. Then there is Robert McGinnis, who willingly shared his wealth of accumulated knowledge regarding the cemeteries of Knoxville, Kathryn M Brown who made available a copy of the only known painting of Knoxville's foundry, Carol Moore who continues to mail timely bulletins regarding the renewed historical interest in the Coal Creek area and, above all, Barry K Thacker PE, founder of the Coal Creek Watershed Foundation, whose achievements are outlined in an appendix at the end of chapter 6.

Eirug Davies
May 2012

CHAPTER 1

The Earlier Welsh Presence

Pre-statehood

NINETY-FIVE COUNTIES MAKE UP the state of Tennessee, and three have been named after individuals of Welsh background, viz., Lewis County which acknowledges Meriwether Lewis for having made it across the continent before anybody else; Morgan County, named after General Daniel Morgan of revolutionary fame and who probably was related to the Siôn ap Rhydderch who compiled a Welsh dictionary in 1725; and then there is Shelby County, which honours Kentucky's first Governor. It is more than likely that the first Welsh person to have ventured into what is now known as Tennessee (and that well before statehood), was Evan Shelby, father of the last mentioned. He had emigrated from the market town of Tregaron as a sixteen year-old in 1735. Although a few others had preceded him by taking up residence in the vicinity of the Holston River in 1768, the earliest surviving document regarding this particular settlement is a letter in his hand that was sent to his children on 3 January 1771. The letter 'f' in the Welsh language is more akin to the English 'v', it seems that he has adhered to the Welsh practice of using the letter 'ff' for the 'f' sound: "Dr Children This is Too lit you know that we are all saffe arrived at our habitation on Holson [River] after a Jurney of three weeks and three days…"

In the following year he was ready to bring his entire family down from Maryland and in doing so he took advantage of the opportunity to transport a variety of goods which could be sold on arrival. These ranged from blankets to boots and cooking utensils and amongst his potential buyers were well-known pioneers such as Valentine Sevier, younger brother of Tennessee's first Governor, John Sevier and Daniel Boone. The last named was Welsh on his mother's side – his father having married a Sarah Morgan whose family had emigrated from Bala, Wales in 1691. Their marriage had taken place on 13 June 1720 at the Welsh Quaker Meeting House in Gwynedd, Pennsylvania.

Years after those pioneering days and with the country caught up in the Revolution by then, Evan Shelby would respond to Patrick Henry's plea that he should arrange for the protection of the more westerly settlers. At the instigation of the British, the Indians had taken to harassing them and, with a contingent of several hundred volunteers, Shelby succeeded in 1779 in subduing the hostile Chickamauga tribe in the vicinity of present-day Chattanooga. Under the heading 'Chickamauga Fight of 1779', and on the 150th anniversary of the occasion in 1929, the *New York Times* set about renewing interest in his exploits:

> The British commanders, with clever strategy, had massed quantities of goods, ammunition, money and weapons on the banks of the Tennessee River and Chickamauga Creek, and Governor Hamilton of Detroit had called a great convention of all the hostile Indian tribes to be held there… but the success of the American expedition under Colonel Shelby prevented all of this… In all, eleven towns were destroyed. The volunteers captured horses, cattle, guns, ammunition and supplies of goods and the stores and money provided by the British for distribution amongst the Indians… he [Shelby] held a sale of the captured horses and supplies. The little stream and the town which subsequently was established near it bear to this day the name Sale Creek.

Little did he realize that three-quarters of a century later, this would be the very place that his fellow countrymen would first avail themselves to Tennessee's coal deposits. Evan Shelby is also reputed to have been one of the first Europeans to traverse across what was to become Knox County. As appealing as this area might have appeared for settlement, the Appalachian Mountains hindered any rapid westward expansion, and it would take until 1796 before the population of Tennessee was deemed sufficient to warrant its inclusion in the Union.

Amongst those spirited enough to acquire land beyond the settlements of the day was a son of Evan Shelby, who bore the same name as his father. He eventually settled some 50 miles north-west of the present-day Nashville. Also to settle about the same distance from Nashville, but in a south-westerly direction, was a Gen. Richard Winn, who had taken part in the ill-fated attempt of defending Charleston during the Revolution. His family had first emigrated to Fauquier County, Virginia in the 1740s and they were reputed to be from the same family as the John Wynne who had been appointed Bishop of St Asaph's in 1715 (it should be noted that gwyn, the Welsh word for white, is often used as a boy's name, either as Gwyn, Wyn or Wynne, but it is only its feminine equivalent, Gwen or Gwyneth, which has gained general acceptance outside Wales itself). Two of the five sons born to the family whilst still in Virginia would move to South Carolina, and it was through their prominence there that the town of Winnsboro was so named. When Gen. Richard Winn eventually relocated to Duck River, Tennessee in 1813, he became the highest ranking soldier to accept land in Tennessee for his wartime services.

Not long afterwards, in 1821, four families from the Welsh Tredyffrin Church in Philadelphia caught a glimpse of Knoxville. Under the leadership of their pastor, a Rev. Thomas Roberts, they were on their way to help the Cherokee Indians in the remotest region of western North Carolina. Travelling with him, in four Conestoga wagons pulled by six horses each, were a school master, a blacksmith and a farmer. They were faced with having to endure an 800 mile journey, and once beyond Knoxville according to the Rev. Thomas Roberts, the land became so infertile that they could barely sustain the horses. Worse was to come on approaching the Smoky Mountains and, despite the worsening terrain and the perils involved in getting the wagons through, it must have been nothing short of a thrilling adventure for the 16 children who accompanied their parents. Another son of the school master, who was born later, became so proficient in the Cherokee language that he often showed a preference for conversing in it. In the meantime, his father had become so closely associated with Chief John Ross, that during the period leading up to the Cherokee removal he was periodically forced to leave the north-western part of North Carolina and seek refuge in Tennessee.

Samuel Roberts

By the mid 19th century, as widespread as the Welsh immigration to America had become, very few were prepared to venture into the more southern states. On Tennessee's northern border, and predating it as a state by four years, was Kentucky. Despite being favourably viewed in Morgan John Rhys's *Darluniad Byr o Kentucky* [A Short Depiction of Kentucky] which was published in 1794 (and within two years of achieving statehood), not many were enticed to even venture there. Over the next three-quarters of a century, the overwhelming tendency amongst the Welsh was to restrict themselves to the more northerly part of the country, whether it would be as industrial workers or those who pioneered different agricultural communities as the country expanded westward. Such farming communities, where the Welsh language prevailed for two or three generations, were invariably located in northern states such as Ohio, Wisconsin, Minnesota and Kansas.

About the only exception to the above was a group led by the already mentioned Samuel Roberts who were struggling to start a farming community in Tennessee just prior to the Civil War. Roberts was a well known and much admired figure in Wales itself. Yet it is doubtful whether anyone who had aspirations about forming a Welsh settlement in the United States could have managed to find a more inappropriate place to settle. Not long after their arrival in 1857, Roberts and his followers, many of whom were from the same Llanbrynmair area, would find themselves subjected to all the horrors of the Civil War. Adding to their misery was a disagreement which had arisen sometime earlier over the ownership of their land and, to make matters even worse, was the fact that not all of it was located in the same general area. From Samuel Roberts's future home at Brynyffynon, which was only ten miles south of the Kentucky border and about eight miles north-west of the small community of Huntsville, it required a journey of around 50 miles towards the south-west before reaching the second part of their holdings. Not that far from there, and located about 60 miles west of Knoxville, was the small town of Crossville and it too was mentioned by Samuel Roberts when he wrote about their recently acquired land. From his comments it appears that he was not particularly deterred by the separation between the two properties:

> Cawsom hefyd y boddhad o glywed Mr Saxton, o New York, yn darlunio i ni ansawdd y tir oeddym wedi brynu ganddo, a'r gofal oedd wedi gymryd i wneuthir i fyny y "diffyg mesur" oeddid wedi gael yn rhai o'r lots. Yr oedd yn dda genym ei glywed hefyd yn rhoddi gair mor dda i'r tir a brynasom gan Mr De Cook o Antwerp, i lawr wrth Crossville, a bod yna le mor obeithiol am lwyddiant ein cymdogaeth.
>
> [*We also had the satisfaction of hearing from Mr Saxton, of New York, describing the nature of the land we'd bought off him, and the care he'd taken to make up for the "measuring difficulties" they'd*

encountered with some of the lots. It was also encouraging to hear him putting in a good word about the land we had purchased from Mr De Cook of Antwerp, down by Crossville, and there was such a promising place for the success of our community.]

At the time of writing he had just arrived in Cincinnati and was yet to reach Brynyffynon where his brother had been since the previous year (1856). A more detailed account of his endeavours up to that stage are to be found in a 23-page booklet entitled *Taith o Lanbrynmair i Cincinnati* [A Journey from Llanbrynmair to Cincinnati] that was published in Cincinnati in 1857. He and his compatriots were by no means the only ones to leave Llanbrynmair for America, and nobody was more acutely aware of this than Samuel Roberts himself: "Of those born in Llanbrynmair during the last half century, there are far more presently residing in America than there are in Llanbrynmair" [O'r bobl a anwyd yn Llanbrynmair yn yr hanner can mlynedd olaf, y mae llawer mwy yn awr yn byw yn America nag sydd yn Llanbrynmair]. As to those who had travelled under his guidance, Wilbur S Shepperson goes as far as to suggest in *Tennessee Historical Quarterly,* XVIII, 162, 1969 that their treatment by being Welsh had provided them with an extra incentive for leaving: "But Welshmen suffered the additional discomfiture of having much of their land held by absentee English landlords, of being forced to support an alien religious establishment and of finding their language and customs marked as inferior." His assessment is surprisingly similar to the sentiment expressed by Samuel Roberts himself: "Our main reason for leaving – viz., our profound feeling of having long suffered scorn and harm through oppressive and cunning overseers of the inheritance under which we have existed" [Ein prif reswm am ymadael – sef ein teimlad dwys ein bod wedi cael hir ddirmyg a cham gan oruchwylwyr trymion a chyfrwys yr etifeddiaeth oeddym wedi byw arni].

In a letter that Samuel Roberts and a David Price of Dinbych had written to thank the ship's purser for their safe passage across the Atlantic, one can gather that there were around 150 from Wales on this particular voyage. No indication is given as to how many of these would accompany Samuel Roberts to Tennessee, but whatever that might have been when they departed from Liverpool on 6 May 1857, they could soon rejoice on having an additional member. Born to the Llwynyffynon family within three hours of setting sail was a child whose name would reflect the circumstances of his birth, his second given name being that of the ship, *The Circassian*.

Even within a year of their arrival in Tennessee, some had become so distraught with their prospects that they decided to leave. Two of the families from Llanbrynmair itself, William and John Roberts Jones of Tymawr Farm and G Williams of Pentremawr Farm, would abandon their holdings to join relatives who had previously settled in Ohio. Given that they were the ones who had assumed a good part of the burden of co-investing in the land with Samuel Roberts and his brother, this must have come as a bitter blow indeed. The departure of such able farmers was a sure indication that not all was as promising as they had once been led to believe.

Indeed, a brief visit from John Breeze was all that it took to dissuade him from staying and becoming part of the venture. Both he and his wife, Mary Jones of Gelli-dywyll, were from Llanbrynmair and they had migrated as members of the contingent whose intent it was to settle in Tennessee. Breeze soon came to the conclusion that the prospect of forming a viable community where they could live with some degree of comfort was not likely to occur during his lifetime. As a consequence, he departed for Paddy's Run, a Welsh community on the outskirts of Cincinnati where he had already left his family. This place had been successfully settled by others from Llanbrynmair at the very end of the 18th century and from here he set out to explore other parts of Ohio. He eventually settled in

Vanvert, a more recently formed Welsh community, and where he resided until his death in 1878.

More ready to try and make the most of their circumstances in Tennessee was one referred to as Cadwgan Fardd (Cadwgan the bard). It is under this assumed bardic name that he is referred to in the correspondence of the Roberts brothers. The signature that appears on one of his own letters is Dafydd Cadwgan, again without any indication as to what his surname might have been. He had been raised in the county of Glamorgan in the southern part of Wales and, despite his large physical appearance with his weight exceeding 200 pounds, he was considered to be a handsome individual. A poet of some renown, he was also said to be an accomplished historian.

His Tennessee home, Ty'nygelli (house-in-the-grove), was within a quarter of a mile of the Brynyffynon home of Samuel Roberts and, on one of his many visits, he had inquired of Samuel Roberts's brother as to why he no longer produced the odd poem anymore. He responded by stating that all the toil associated with farming a densely wooded area had drained whatever creativity he possessed, and further, he doubted if Cadwgan could do any better. After negotiating a token bet of one fip (a Mexican silver coin worth six cents), Cadwgan instantaneously produced eight stanzas that adhered to all the metrical requirements of traditional Welsh verse. Choosing the window (ffenestr) of the Brynyffynon home as a theme, the first stanza relates as to how the old author (hen awdur) of 'Short Songs' (a reference to a short collection of hymns, *Caniadau Byrion*, that Samuel Roberts had published), was seated nearby, brimming forth with an array of new ideas:

> Yn ffenestr Brynyffynon, – hen awdur
> Y Caniadau Byrion
> Eistedda i lawr yr awr hon,
> Yn ferw o fyfyrion.

Whatever the initial plight of those who decided to remain in Tennessee, it could only get worse for them at the outbreak of the Civil War. Being that they were located in a pro-Union part of what was generally a Confederate state, they could expect very little sympathy and, to make matters even worse, was the fact that Tennessee, as a border state, had to endure more than its share of the fighting. Little could be done to counter the harassment brought about by soldiers constantly on the move:

> Peth cyfyng oedd gorfod cuddio y tri mochyn tewion mewn cut yng nghwr y dyrus goed, allan o gyrraedd y Secesh, ond yng nghyrraedd lladroniaid creulawn y goedwig. Peth cyfyng oedd gorfod goddef i ddau leidr diog gymryd y tewaf o'r moch, a hynny ganol dydd, i gael porc rhad i'w teulu carpiog. Peth cyfyng oedd gorfod cymryd y ddau arall yn ôl i'w cut wrth y tŷ, o gyrraedd lladron y coed, i gyrraedd gwibiaid y Secesh. Peth cyfyng oedd gorfod claddu yn y ddaear, dro ar ôl tro, bethau fel pridd enaid o ymenyn, a chafnaid o gig, a chelyrnaid o flawd...

> [*How restrictive it was having to hide the three fattened pigs in a pen that bordered on the confusing woods, out of the reach of the Secesh, but within reach of the cruel thieves of the forest. How restrictive it was having to endure two lazy thieves taking the fattest of the pigs, and that in the middle of the day, to get cheap pork for their ragged clad family. How restrictive it was having to take the other two back to their pen by the house, out of reach of the forest thieves, but within reach of the wandering Secesh. How restrictive it was having to bury underground, time after time, things like butter, a trough of meat, a tub full of flour...*]

So, from being a prolific writer who had once raised the social awareness of Wales, here was Samuel Roberts left isolated from his readership, and with his energies often diverted to worrying over something as mundane as the destiny of three over-nourished pigs. Yet when he first arrived in Tennessee, one gets a glimpse of his humanitarian leanings through his efforts to promote a 'unifying' railroad link between north and south. From his perspective this could have led to a better understanding between the two sides who would eventually find themselves locked in a bitter conflict. Between 1858 and 1860 he made his thoughts known through a series of articles published in a variety of regional newspapers, as well as in the *Rail Road Magazine*:

> I never think of the country between Knoxville, Tennessee and Lexington, Kentucky, without astonishment that there is, as yet, no midland connection between the Railways of the North and the Railways of the South... [America] has allowed a narrow strip of land to stretch its ugly length for more than 500 miles along the boundary of its two oldest states, across the very centre of the country, between the North and the South; and she has, as yet, attempted no railway cutting across it! Should the midland population on each side of that idle strip of land attempt to traffic together, or to carry on any description commerce or intercourse, they must make a circuit of more than a thousand miles, around its Atlantic end, or around its Mississippi end. Whereas, if there had been a midland railway across the small of its back, the distance would have been less than two hundred miles... The completion of that connecting link would be a new bond of Union, of undying strength, around the very centre of the country... It would be a kind of electric medium for the virtues of the North to flow down to the South, and for the graces of the South to flow up to the North, and both sides would be greatly gainers by such an admixture. It would convey produce from the South that would be of important value to the North, and would convey produce from the North that would be most useful to the South...

Despite his early enthusiasm for furthering the cause of his adopted country, by 1867, and after ten frustrating years in Tennessee, he had lost the will to remain at Brynyffynon. He and his followers would return to a Wales that still suffered from all the ills that no other public figure would have dared to express:

> Thousands of them have given of the strength of their days to their masters for nothing but their food. They are poorer to-day after all their labour and care than they were thirty years ago. The landlords treat them as slaves. The serfs of Russia, however oppressed, have earned more the last forty years than the majority of tenant farmers of the highlands of Wales. The landlords of Wales are no better than the Barons of Russia. Soon the land will be deserted. No one will remain to cultivate it but parsons, beggars, stewards, turncoats, gamekeepers and bailiffs.

As to their misfortune in Tennessee, not all of the blame rests on the leadership of Samuel Roberts himself. While the tendency in Wales is to attribute their lack of success to deception on the part of the land brokers, Samuel Roberts does not appear to have been particularly well advised by a relative of his and a former Governor of Ohio, William Bebb. As the State's first native-born Governor, he should have been far more astute when it came to assessing the potential and the likelihood of success with their purchase. Added to that were the ramifications of going to a slave State, something that was so abhorrent to Samuel Roberts himself (for a recent discussion of some of his ideals, see D Williams's article in a 2004 issue of *Taliesin*). It is not unreasonable to think that cousin William Bebb had encouraged the endeavour from the very beginning, and from what can be gleaned from his correspondence with President Lincoln, it appears that he may have even joined them in Tennessee at one stage. Left financially ruined as a result of his involvement, his letter to Lincoln on 12 June 1861 makes a rather pathetic plea for a position in his administration, a favour expected in lieu of having campaigned on his behalf during the election:

Most of my co-labourers in the West have been remembered Corwin, Smith, Bates, Judd, Schurz, Carter, Schenck, Holloway, Dole, Clay, Edmunds &c. While others such as Browning, Davis are reserved I hope for higher honours on the Bench. Am I alone to be ignored? You know I entered the canvass with your approbation. You know I thereby lost my home, practice house, furniture, library, wardrobe *all* in Tennessee. You know my family are at Springfield dependent on their children for a house to cover them… If you can not give me one place you can another. A word from you will more than compensate for all our losses and save a worthy family. You may get a more able but not a more faithful public servant − or more devoted personal friend.

By the end of 1861 William Bebb would be in Washington working as a lowly clerk in the Patent Office. As to those who saw no alternative but to return to Wales, if only they had heeded the advice of another long-time Ohio resident, the Rev. Ben Chidlaw. In 1856, and a year prior to their arrival, he had openly opposed their proposed settlement in Tennessee. This he had made known through the pages of the monthly publication *Y Cenhadwr Americanaidd* [The American Missionary]:

> … rhaid iddynt ddodi *padlock* ar eu tafodau, byw ynghanol yr aflan beth, heb ddweud gair yn ei erbyn. Gwell lle, can waith gwell, ar faesydd toreithiog Kansas, neu yn nyffrynoedd Nebraska. Hyderaf y bydd i'r bobl annwyl, eu gwell ni ddaeth i'n gwlad, ystyried yn ddifrifol yr anhawsderau o sefydlu mewn talaith gaeth a mwynhau eu hiawnderau anwylaf…

> [… *they'll have to place a padlock on their tongues, be forced to live under demeaning circumstances, without uttering a single objection. Better, a hundred times better, would be the fertile meadows of Kansas or the valleys of Nebraska. I trust that these dear people, whose better never made it to our country, will seriously consider the difficulties of settling in a slave state while yet enjoying their own dearest rights…*]

Samuel Roberts's pacifist tendencies had also alienated him from the majority of Welsh Americans who saw no resolution to the slave issue short of an armed conflict. As already indicated, the more recently arrived Welsh immigrants were invariably located in the northern states and many considered it their duty to join the Union Army. As will be seen later, many of those who were exposed to Tennessee under the worst of circumstances could still recognise its potential and be drawn back after the war was over.

Civil War Participation

Typical of the many who saw service in Tennessee during the Civil War was Owen Griffith, a captain with the 22nd from Wisconsin. Alongside him when he had the misfortune of being captured in the vicinity of Nashville was another Welsh soldier who, accidentally, brought about his own death: "while he was destroying his gun all its blast went to his thigh. Around 9 o'clock that night the doctors in Nashville removed his thigh, and he died around 12 o'clock that night" [wrth dorri ei ddryll aeth yr ergyd i gyd i'w glun. Y noson honno tua 9 o'r gloch darfu i'r meddygon yn Nashville dorri ei glun, a bu farw tua 12 o'r gloch y noswaith honno].

Others were to participate in another series of battles that were fought in the vicinity of Chattanooga towards the end of 1863. One such individual, Owen R Jones, had been born in Anglesey, Wales in 1835 and had emigrated to Minnesota in 1855. Compounding the difficulty of interpreting the handwritten letter sent to inform his relatives of his well-being, is the fact that he used no punctuation whatsoever. After briefly mentioning his present circumstances he goes on to discuss his aspirations on returning to Minnesota:

> … mae yn ddiamau eich bod yn hysbys o'r ymladdfa galad sudd wedi ei hymladd ein hun. Gallaf eich hysbysebu fy mod

wedi bod yn [?] dostiri yn anfeidrol trwy yr holl beryglion
fel na chawdd yr un niwed gyffwrdd a fy mhabell. Yr wyf yn
ceisio cydnabod yr arglwydd am ei ofal mawr am danaf. Mae
ein byddin wedi bod yn orchfygol ar bob point. Yr ydym wedi
cymryd tua 2,700[0?] yn garcharorion a thua 52 canons. Ni
tydi ddim iws i mi dreio rhoi yr hanes i chwi o ran mi. Rydych
wedi gwelad yn y papurau yr holl hanes [?] hun… mi rwyf
yn meddwl os bydd i fy hon dal a fy iechid gael ei cadw tan
mis Awst am brynu tim o geffyla a wagan a dod i Minnesota
yn y ffol ac os gallaf gael pisin o dir yn agos i chwi mi dreiaf ei
gael ond os na allaf mi rwuf yn meddwl y gallaf wneud gwell
bywoliaeth yn Minnesota hefo tim o geffyla cryfion nac wrth
weithio wrth y mis…

[… for sure you are aware of the hard battle that was fought by us.
I can assure you that I have been through all the dangers mercifully
beyond measure so no harm came by way of my encampment. I am
trying to acknowledge the lord for his great caring over me. Our army
has been victorious on every point. We have taken about 2,700[0?]
as prisoners and about 52 cannons. It is of no use for me to attempt
to give you an account from my part. You have seen all the facts in
the papers… I have been thinking should I last and my health holds
until August, of buying a team of horses and a wagon and to come to
Minnesota in the Fall if I can get a piece of land near you. I'll try and
get it but if I fail I think I can make a better living in Minnesota with
a team of strong horses than through working by the month…]

At the end of his letter he also expresses his desire to join his
relatives for a return visit to the 'old country'. Less evident were
those of Welsh background who had been in the country for
several generations and whose allegiance was firmly rooted in the
South. Often they were descended from families whose presence
could be traced back to colonial times and one such individual
was an Edward Thomas who was destined to inherit the family's
3,000-acre plantation some 40 miles south of Savannah, Georgia.
Born in 1840, he was a descendant of the John Thomas who

is credited as being the captain of the very first vessel to bring colonists to Georgia. Still to be seen on current maps of Georgia is the so-named Thomas Landing and it was there that Edward Thomas ran the family plantation with its 125 slaves. Despite showing a certain degree of compassion towards them, that was not the case when it came to foraging for supplies in Tennessee and on having to force the likes of Samuel Roberts to give up whatever little they had:

> I remember going into a flour mill in Tennessee and asking for a certain amount of wheat flour, which the miller promptly furnished, and then, of course, wanted his pay. He would only receive my "promise to pay" after it was stuck on my sword and I quietly but determinedly let him feel how sharp it was when pressed against his abundant stomach. Then after getting the flour, how to prepare it for food? Found a lot of large flat stones, which I had the men heat very hot, and mixing the flour with water in a large barrel, spread it over the stones, and thus we had very large pones of eatable stuff. These, in large hunks, were handed the troopers as they rode by, and all shouting "Hurrah for Captain Thomas".

Among those resident in Tennessee who were left to face the aftermath of the war were descendants of a Robin ap Robin Jones who had been born in Sussex County, Virginia but had subsequently moved to North Carolina. There his son, Allen Jones, had become one of the five to be appointed by that state as a brigadier general in 1776. Later a granddaughter of his named Mary Rebecca Long would marry William Julious Polk (his cousin was to become president) and in 1828 they moved to Columbia, Tennessee. It was their daughter, Mary Jones Polk Branch, who was left to ponder over the family's future:

> The war had ended – the long agony was over, and again we met in our mother's home, in Columbia, Tennessee. First came Lucius, bravest of the brave, on crutches. Next, Cadwalader,

whose horse was shot from under him, and he left for dead on
the battlefield at Prairie Grove. Next, Rufus, who spent his
seventeenth birthday in a prison on Johnson's Island.

Oh, the horrors of civil war! My mother was a Spartan
mother, and she said to her four boys, "Go and do your duty".
There was my gay and handsome brother, Tom, who left his
wife and children; Lucius, whose name I can not write without
a pang; … Colonel Cadwalader, who was first with Jackson in
Virginia, afterwards in the western army under General Price;
promoted for gallantry from second lieutenant to colonel. At
the battle of Prairie Grove he was left for dead on the field,
taken to the Federal Hospital, and a month afterwards liberated
in an exchange of prisoners. Capt. Rufus Julius… was a
prisoner on his eighteenth [?] birthday at Johnson's Island. He
was in the last skirmish of the war in Alabama.

Cadwalader is another of the distinctive Welsh names and
the 'ap' designation, which had been forced out of use through
having to comply with the English record-keeping system, seems
to have resurfaced with this family right up to Mary Jones Polk
Branch's generation: "my mother's nephew, Robin ap C Jones,
was one of the loveliest characters I have ever known, and the
dearest friend of my life." The 'ap' implies that someone is the
son of the person whose name appears immediately afterwards
and it serves as the equivalent of 'Mac' which is so prevalent with
Irish and Scottish derived names.

Probably the most praiseworthy of all the Welsh to venture
into Tennessee during the Civil War was the Rev. D W
Phillips who had left Boston for Nashville in 1864. He had first
arrived in the country as a youngster in 1829, travelling in the
company of one of the deacons of Rhydwilym Baptist Church in
Pembrokeshire, Wales, and his initial intent was to stay just long
enough to become proficient in the English language. Instead of
returning he continued his education and, as a devout Baptist,
he enrolled at Brown University, the first college to be affiliated

with the denomination and located in Providence, Rhode Island. While there he managed to support himself through preaching on Sundays and after graduating in 1837 he served as pastor to different churches just north of Boston.

As the Civil War progressed he had the foresight to mull over what could best be done to improve the well-being of slaves once left free. On reaching Nashville he took it upon himself to educate them as best he could, doing so while providing for himself through preaching to a white congregation on Sundays. After initially using his own home as a classroom, he managed to obtain the use of a hall associated with an African-American congregation and his efforts eventually led to the founding of The Nashville Normal and Theological Institute in 1866. Ten years later it was moved from the city's centre to its outskirts and for over a quarter of a century Dr D W Phillips continued to devote all his energy and time to instruct former slaves into becoming teachers and ministers. The ridicule often directed at his own cultural background in Wales would have undoubtedly placed him in a better position to appreciate some of the difficulties encountered by his students. Still fresh on his mind was how he himself had been taught to read on his mother's knee, confined to a single textbook and without knowing the name of a single letter. His lone textbook had been the sixteenth-century translation of the Welsh Bible, and while it might not have always succeeded in saving his countrymen's souls, it did manage to put many of them on the path to literacy.

CHAPTER 2

The Industrial Background

From Wales to Pennsylvania

By the beginning of the 20th century more than a quarter of a million of Wales's total population of two million would be working undergound. The coal industry had experienced a period of unprecedented growth over the better part of the previous century and around 600 mines could be found in the country's southern valleys. On taking a closer look at the two adjoining valleys of Rhondda Fach (small) and Rhondda Fawr (big), one finds that their combined population had increased from around 500 in 1801 to well in excess of 150,000 just over a century later. Something in excess of 50 mines were to be found in these two valleys alone and a signifcant number of them provided work for a thousand or more miners.

One of the better-known mines in Wales, the so-called Big Pit in Blaenafon was in recent years designated as a World Heritage Site. Maintained by former miners as part of the National Museum of Wales, one can take the 300-foot plunge down the main shaft and follow along where some of its 1,300 miners had once laboured under exceedingly difficult and dangerous conditions. The early development of this particular region, with its ready supply of wood, coal, limestone and iron ore typified what took place in other parts of south Wales as well. Starting in 1787, and without any capital available in Wales itself, three Englishmen took it upon themselves to lease a seven-mile strip of land from the Marquis of Abergavenny. After forcing the local farmers off their land two years later they managed to produce their first pig iron. By 1796 the annual production at this site had reached 5,500 tons. Such early endeavours at producing iron usually depended on charcoal for heating the admixture of ores, and it was only after the countryside had become denuded of trees that coal, together with the coke derived from it, became of such importance. In Blaenafon itself, its days as an iron producer came to an end in 1904, but the coal mining activities continued until 1980. By then the so-called Big Pit had been in operation for a full century.

Of considerable significance in Wales's industrial development was the opening of the Glamorgan Canal in 1794. This enabled Merthyr to develop into one of the world's leading iron producers and for Cardiff to become a leading export port. Located in Merthyr was the renowned Cyfarthfa Works and together with an operation of similar magnitude in nearby Dowlais, the area could more than match the output of any place in Europe. Ultimately, coal mining would surpass the production of iron in importance and, based on the tonnage of coal being shipped, Cardiff was to become a busier port than even London or Liverpool.

For the better part of the 19th century Pennsylvania benefited from the presence of a large contingent of experienced Welsh miners and iron workers. Starting in the eastern part of the state with the coal mining operations at Carbondale and Pottsville, their impact would be felt as far west as the iron and steel mills that subsequently came into being in Johnstown and Pittsburgh. From the two and a half million tons of coal extracted within the state in 1846, the output continued to grow until it became comparable to what was being mined in Wales itself – the total reached around 50 million tons by the turn of the century. The most significant of Pennsylvania's anthracite coal regions was the one that extended from Carbondale to Wilkes-Barre and flourishing within this one region alone were over 50 Welsh-language churches.

The individual tasked with purifying the initial pig iron, and thereby ensuring that the resulting wrought iron would display the most desirable of properties, was the so-called 'puddler'. By itself Pittsburgh could lay claim to having as many as two dozen Welsh master puddlers and in a well-known novel from the period, *Life in the Iron Mills*, Rebecca Davis acknowledges their presence somewhat further downstream in Wheeling, West Virginia: "The old man, like many of the puddlers and feeders of the mills was Welsh… " The following, written by one so employed in the vicinity of Pittsburgh, gives a graphic description of what it took to be a puddler:

> The puddling furnace has a working door on a level with a man's stomach… It is a porthole opening upon a sea of flame… Through this working door I put in the charge of *pigs* that were to be boiled. These short pieces of mill iron had been smelted from iron ore; they had taken the first step on their journey from wild iron to civilized iron … Vigorously I stroked that fire for thirty minutes with dampers open and the draft roaring while the pig-iron melted down like ice cream under an electric fan… There were five bakings every day and this meant the shoveling in of nearly two tons of coal. In summer I was stripped to the waist and panting while the sweat poured down across my heavy muscles… What time I was not stroking, I was stirring the charge with a long iron rabble that weighed some twenty-five pounds… The melted iron contains carbon, sulphur and phosphorus, and to get rid of them, especially the sulphur and phosphorus, is the object of all this heat and toil… My purpose in slackening my heat as soon as the pig-iron was melted was to oxidize the phosphorus and sulphur ahead of the carbon… When this reaction begins I see light flames breaking through the lake of molten slag in my furnace. Probably from

> such a sight as this the old-time artists got their pictures of
> Hell... The purpose now is to oxidize the carbon, too, without
> reducing the phosphorus and sulphur and causing them to
> return to the iron...

As well as being physically demanding, the task called for a great deal of guile and judgement on the part of the puddler. The above account comes from a James John Davis who had left Tredegar in Wales as a seven year-old in 1880. His family had settled in Sharon, Ohio, and when twelve years old he had started working in the mills alongside his father. Intermixed with many of his descriptions of the hardships encountered in the mills are references to frequent visits he would later make to the White House. As unlikely as it seems, he was singled out by President Harding to become a member of his cabinet, serving as Secretary of Labour.

Despite their British background, many arrived with only a scant knowledge of English. In his memoirs one well-respected Congregational Minister admitted to having lived in New York City for three years before even attempting to become bilingual. This linquistic transition was eased by their tendency to settle together, be it in the industrialized areas of Pennsylvania or within the farming communities created further west. This, undoubtedly, would have provided newcomers with a degree of comfort whilst adjusting to their new environment. Keeping them informed of both the major issues of the day and what was transpiring within their own communities were a limited number of Welsh-language monthly magazines and weekly newspapers. Starting around 1840, these were published on their behalf in such places as Utica, New York and Pottsville, Pennsylvania.

Included from time to time in such publications were biographical sketches of earlier Welsh immigrants who had given their all to the Revolution and the country's early development. Proud of their Celtic heritage as they were, this would have given the more recent arrivals a sense of belonging and amongst those elaborated on were the likes of Generals Evan and Isaac Shelby, with the latter being largely responsible for the victory at King's Mountain. Had Patrick Henry not requested that the father Evan was needed to take care of the western frontier, he would have almost certainly travelled to Boston to aid Washington with the organization of the Continental Army. There in Boston as it was were General Daniel Morgan, General Otho Williams and the John Morgan who was to become the army's physician-in-chief. Two members of Philadelphia's Welsh Society had risked everything by signing the Declaration of Independence and, as Secretary of the Treasury, a third society member by the name of Samuel Meredith had used his personal wealth to keep the country afloat after the revolution. While it is questionable whether every one of their new-found heroes were of Welsh descent, many of the accounts were as factual and as concisely written as what would later appear about such individuals in the *Dictionary of American Bibliography*. This new-found pride accounts, in part, for the exceptionally high percentage of Welsh immigrants who saw to it to become citizens. For those who would subsequently move to Tennessee, and whatever adjustments that lay ahead, they would be relatively minor compared to what they had already faced whilst in Pennsylvania.

Industrial Activity in Pre-War Tennessee

With the demise of the old southern plantations after the Civil War, the South was faced with having to turn towards a more industrialized world as found in the North. It was only then that many of Pennsylvania's Welsh became aware of the benefits to be gained by moving south and where their skills and know-how would once more prove of value. Having brought Tennessee to their attention was the local knowledge attained through a handful of their fellow countrymen who had participated in one of the pre-war attempts at industrialization. Dating from the 1850s, this particular effort seems to have been dominated by a number of ill-fated attempts at getting a certain iron mill to operate successfully. As this mill would again feature in much of what transpired immediately after the Civil War, it becomes of interest to take a further look at its earlier history and the few Welsh individuals who had struggled in vain to make it commercially viable.

The mill had its origins in Danville, Pennsylvania, from where it had been transported by sea to Charleston, South Carolina and then overland by barge and railroad until it reached the small town of Loudon (or Lauden), 30 miles south-west of Knoxville. Somehow the citizens had bought the mill under the assumption that they could profit by selling house lots to those attracted to the town by the prospect of employment. However, operating the mill proved to be far more difficult than envisioned, and by 1863 they were probably glad to see the last of it when it was removed to Knoxville. This was not done by the Confederates, as is often thought, but by an individual named Samuel Atkins who had acquired it from the Lauden Town Company. Although one Welsh-language account mentions that he ran it to the "advantage of the Confederates", it was soon taken over by the Union Army. At the conclusion of the war it fell into the possession of one of their former officers, a Col. H S Chamberlain.

Before its removal to Knoxville, and right from the time it was first brought to Louden, the mill had been plagued by one difficulty after another. The initial failures were hardly improved upon with the arrival of three experienced northern workers in Evan Howells, Daniel Williams and Abraham Cooper. Again not much progress was made after a Rees Lloyd had travelled from Pittsburgh itself, bringing with him another highly experienced worker. Hindering all their efforts was the lack of a nearby supply of iron ore and coal, and that in the days prior to the railroad and when the roads remained in a pitiful condition. Then to arrive from Ironton, Ohio in 1857 were John H Jones, Thomas Harris and David Phillips, and while the last named left soon afterwards, the other two persevered and eventually achieved a certain degree of success. Thomas Harris managed to start a new coal mine at the same Sale Creek as where Evan Shelby had held his sale and, though not particularly close by, it appears that its coal proved to be more advantageous. Once the war broke out neither of the two were prepared to stay and, as a consequence, they set out to make their way "over the mountains and through the woods in a northern direction without ever returning again to Lauden" [dros y mynyddoedd a thrwy y coedwigoedd i gyfeiriad y gogledd ac ni ddychwelasant mwyach i Lauden].

As was the case here, other unrelated efforts also struggled during their formative years. With the Tennessee Coal, Iron and Railroad Co., it was initially organized under the name of Sewanee Mining Co. in 1852, and that after coal had been discovered in the vicinity of Tracy City some 20–30 miles north-west of Chattanooga. Under construction at the time was a railroad line that was to link Nashville to Chattanooga, and in 1858 a branch line was added that led directly to the mine. As advantageous as this was, they were often left unable to sell more than a car load or two daily. This led to financial difficulties and, in 1860, they re-emerged from bankruptcy under the name of Tennessee Coal & Railroad Co. Then in 1861, and on being seized by the Confederate Army, their rolling stock was removed. By the following year their remaining assets would be in Union hands and whatever ambitions they had for producing iron would have to wait until well after the Civil War.

Another Chattanooga area enterprise to have its progress disrupted by the war was the East Tennessee Iron Company. They had operated a foundry from as early as 1853, and by 1856 the so-called Bluff Furnace was turning out 172 tons of pig iron annually. In 1859 they opted for converting the furnace to run on coke rather than charcoal, but between teething troubles and the outbreak of the war, it appears that they never fully met expectations.

Possibly involved with the above conversion was the William Richard Jones who later on would oversee the operations of the Edgar Thomson Steel Co. some 10 miles east of Pittsburgh. He also acted as a consultant to Carnegie, Phipps & Co. and after one periodic visit he was described as "probably the greatest mechanical genius that ever entered the Carnegie Shops". He was the son of the Rev. John G Jones who had left Wales for Pennsylvania in 1832. Without specifying what company he worked for, one report described how, "In 1859 he went to Chattanooga, Tennessee, where he assisted Miles Edwards in the erection of a blast furnace. He remained in the South until after the breaking out of the Rebellion, having meanwhile married Miss Harriet Lloyd, of Chattanooga." After his eventual departure he served as a captain in the Union Army.

As such early attempts at producing iron in the Chattanooga area were not particularly flourishing, Tennessee never became a major supplier to the Confederate cause. Instead, it appears that they were left with having to rely on what could be produced either in Virginia or Alabama (see Anne Knowles in *Technology and Culture*, 42, 1–26, 2001). From an industrial perspective the net effect of the war was to delay the area's industrial advancement and one can presume that far more progress would have been made had such highly capable individuals as William Richard Jones and John H Jones remained in Chattanooga and Lauden.

As to the previously mentioned Tennessee Coal, Iron and Railroad Co., it would take until 1881 before they managed to produce iron for the first time. It was only then that their first blast furnace became operational 20 miles west of Chattanooga. About the only advancement that occured during the war itself was the rolling mill, started in 1864 by the Federal Government, and for the specific purpose of straightening out rails that had been removed and twisted by Confederate troops. This particular mill would later become part of the Roane Iron Company and this is what enabled it to expand so successfully into the Chattanooga area. As will be seen later, many of its key workers could also claim to have a Welsh background.

Not all of the limited numbers of Welshmen found in Tennessee prior to the war were involved with the extraction of coal and iron ore. The north-western part of Wales was as noted for its slate as south Wales was for its coal, and any efforts at quarrying would be expected to involve slate rather than the marble which later proved to be of greater significance. Whilst it is unclear whether any attempts were made at operating a slate quarry prior to the war, one ill-fated attempt at finding a suitable quarry site came as late as 1895. If nothing else, an account related to this effort gives an interesting insight into the way of life of those inhabitants who lived in the rugged Madisonville area south of Knoxville (see appendix at the end of this chapter).

A few others had become involved with the mining of zinc but again it isn't clear when such an effort got under way. Still to be found about 20 miles up from Knoxville as late as the 1890s were a few Welshmen who had been there from the start of the metal's extraction. More specific information exists regarding those whose background proved invaluable to the state's fledgling copper industry. The Swansea area in Wales was noted for its unique way of processing copper and so it comes as no surprise to find that a limited number from that area could be found near Tennessee's southern border and where the metal was being extracted. Located approximately 50 miles east of Chattanooga, their progress was hindered by the remoteness of the place. As they might have arrived somewhat earlier than Samuel Roberts and his followers, they could very well be the first collective group from Wales to have settled in Tennessee:

Bu yma Gymry yn cloddio a thoddi rhwd-efydd (copr) cyn
y rhyfel yn Ducktown. Mri William Edwards a Thomas
Merchant o ardal Abertawe, ddechreuasant y gwaith hwnnw.
Dygodd y mwn copr yn Ducktown amryw o Gymry i'r ardal
honno cyn y rhyfel; ond mae yr oll erbyn heddiw [1892] wedi
ymwasgaru drwy wahanol ranau o Tennessee a Georgia. Y
llynedd yr ymadewodd y Cymro olaf, sef Mr. Edward Morgan,
o'r lle. Mae "gwyr y wlad hon" erbyn heddiw, wedi eu dysgu
gan Gymry, yn medru cloddio a thoddi copr cystal a hwythau.

[*There were Welshmen here in Ducktown before the war digging
and smelting copper. Those works were started by Messrs William
Edwards and Thomas Merchant from the Swansea area. The copper
ore in Ducktown attracted many Welshmen to that area before the
war; but by today [1892] all of them have scattered to different parts
of Tennessee and Georgia. It was last year that the last of the Welsh,
Mr Edward Morgan, left the place. By now those from this country
have learnt from the Welsh, and are as capable as them in extracting
the copper.*]

As to the coal miners themselves, about the earliest to practice
his skills in Tennessee was the Cwmllyfnell-born Rees Rees.
According to a Rev. T D Thomas who was to stay with him
during a short visit from Iowa in 1891, "Mr Rees was amongst
the first to come and open a coal mine in Tennessee" [Yr oedd
Mr Rees ymhlith y cyntaf a ddaeth i agor gwaith glo i Tennessee].
It appears that he had worked in the previously mentioned Sale
Creek from as early as 1857 and it was only much later that he
had moved to the nearby Soddy. Also having worked at both
places was the Llanstephan-born Thomas W Price, who had
been raised nevertheless in Cwmbach near Aberdare. He did not
emigrate until much later, and with the country caught up in the
Civil War by the time of his arrival in 1862, his initial years were
spent in Ohio.

As influential as anybody when it came to the Welsh influx
after the Civil War was the previously mentioned Llandybie-

born John H Jones. Through his involvement in Lauden just prior to the outbreak of hostilities, he was well positioned to send Joseph Richards a letter outlining the mill's potential. This was what prompted Joseph Richards to travel from Harrisburg, Pennsylvania and examine the mill in Knoxville. To one of his experience it was immediately apparent that they were never likely to succeed and as one of his compatriots would later reaffirm, "poor fellows, not one of them understood a thing as to how to make iron" [*poor fellows*, nid oedd yr un ohonynt yn deall dim am y ffordd i wneud haearn]. It was Joseph Richards's commitment to ensure the successful operation of this particular mill that prompted others to follow.

Thirty miles north-west of Knoxville, and in a hilly location that was initially known as Coal Creek, they discovered the coal required for running the mill. This locality, together with the Mechanicsville section of Knoxville, can be regarded as one of the three principal regions where the Welsh would excel after the war. Another area of Welsh concentration would be centered on Chattanooga, a good 100 miles to the south-west of Knoxville, and many would hold key positions in the city's leading iron producing companies. Relativily close by was the coal mining district of Soddy – a place that was more readily reached in its earlier days through taking a barge from Chattanooga and following the Tennessee River northward for a good 20 miles. Towards the end of the century other opportunities were opening up in the vicinity of Jellico at Tennessee's northern border. Though many of its Welsh-related communities would be located just over the state line in Kentucky, it was to Tennessee that they would turn to meet their needs. What follows provides a more detailed account of their post-war involvement at these three locations.

Golwg ar Dyddynwyr Mynyddig

R R Williams

Daeth i'm rhan y flwydd ddiweddaf [1895] i dreulio chwech mis ar fynyddoedd talaith gyfoethog Tennessee, i chwilio rhanau helaeth o'r mynyddoedd a ffurfiant ranau o'r gadwyn fawr a elwir Appalachian, yr hyn sydd yn 1,300 o filltiroedd o hyd. Diau genyf fod yn yr ucheldiroedd anhygyrch hyn drysorau lawer yn cael eu hystorio i'r oesau sydd yn dyfod… ar droed y mynydd lle yr oeddwn yn chwilio am chwarel llechi, y mae y pentref lle gwnawn fy nghartref, er i mi dreulio y rhan fwyaf o lawer o'r chwech mis ar y mynyddoedd, Sul, gwyl a dydd gwaith. Pentref bach digon llwydaidd mewn gwlad amaethyddol, tua hanner can milltir i'r deheuau o Knoxville, ydyw Madisonville, wedi gweled gwell amser, a hynny cyn y *Gwrthryfel Mawr*…

Preswylir y mynyddau cribog a llethrog hyn gan bobl dlodion, a gelwir hwynt yn y wlad o amgylch, *Mynyddwyr*, ac y maent yn ddosbarth o bobl yn preswylio eu hunain, ac wedi bod felly am lawer o genedlaethau. Prif gynyrch eu tyddynod anwastad yn y cilfachau a'r ceunentydd ydyw indrawn, ac y maent yn gwneud eu bywoliaeth bron yn gwbl o gynyrch eu tir. Mae gan bob un o'r tyddynwyr ychydig o greaduriaid ar eu lle – mulod, gwartheg, defaid, da pluog, moch, cwn, a chathod; a rhai ohonynt yn cadw geifr a cheffylau. Prif gynhaliaeth y bobl a'u hanifeiliaid ydyw corn. Corn ydyw pob peth y ffarm, am gorn y disgwylia y mul, gan foelio ei glystiau, a chorn i'r fuwch, ynghyd a'i fodder, corn i'r moch, a chorn a fyn y da pluog, pe rhaid iddynt ei ladrata o'r ysguboriau a'r meusydd. Mae yn eu mysg ddihareb na chlywais i mo honi ond ganddynt hwy. Pan mae un yn gwneud rhywbeth yn led brysur, dywedant ei fod mor brysur a *gwyddau yn pigo corn*. Ceir yma ddigonedd o laeth ac ymenyn cystal ag a geir yn unman yng Nghymru. Gwelir cychod gwenyn bron wrth bob bwthyn…

Mae y mynyddwyr hyn yn bobl heddychol a charedig, ac yn ddiarebol am eu lletygarwch. Un ystafell, fel peth cyffredin, sydd yn eu bwthynod; ychydig o ddodrefn, a'r rhai hynny yn blaen a garw, o wneuthuriad cartref. Ceir dwfr da ym mhob man ar y mynyddoedd, a'r ffrydiau yn heigio o bysgod, ac yn eu plith ceir brithylliaid. Mae y bobl hyn, fel peth cyffredin, yn grefyddol, a chanddynt fan gapeli yn wasgaredig ar y llethrau… Maent yn hynod o anllythrenog; ychydig gyfarfyddir yma yn meddu ar lyfr…

Some observations on the Mountain Dwellers

R R Williams

Last year [1895] it came upon me to spend six months on the mountains located in the rich state of Tennessee, to explore the better part of those mountains which form part of the long chain called Appalachia, and which extend over 1,300 miles. I have little doubt that within this inaccessible and higher type terrain there are many treasures being stored for the ages yet to come… at the foot of the mountain where I was seeking out a slate quarry, was a village where I made my home, though I spent by far the greater part of the six months on the mountains, Sundays, holidays, and work days. Madisonville is a small rather undistinguished village in an agricultural region, fifty miles south of Knoxville, and which had experienced better times, that being before the Great Civil War…

These steeply ridged mountains are occupied by poor people, and they are referred to in the surrounding area as Mountain Men, being a class of people who are self-sufficient, and having been so for several generations. The main product of their small undulating holdings in between the nooks and ravines is corn, and their living comes almost exclusively off the land. Each of the small land holders has a few animals – mules, cattle, sheep, the feathered kind, pigs, dogs and cats; and some keep goats and horses. The main sustenance of both people and animals is corn. Corn is everything on the farm, it is corn that the mule eagerly awaits for, by spreading open his ears, corn to the cow, together with its fodder, corn for the pigs, and it is corn that the feathered ones demand, even if they have to steal it from the barn or fields. They have a proverb which I've never heard of other than through them. When one is profusely involved in some task or other, he is said to be as busy as a goose pecking on corn. Milk and butter are plentiful and as good as can be obtained anywhere in Wales. Beehives are to be seen at practically every dwelling…

These mountain people are both peaceful and kind, and unmatched in their hospitality. One room is the general rule for their dwellings, with very little furniture, and those plain and rough from being home crafted. Good water is obtained everywhere on the mountains, the streams team with fish, and with trout found in their midst. These people are generally religious, with small churches scattered over the sharp inclines… They are illiterate to the extreme, with very few possessing a book…

Travels of David Groves and Cadwgan the Bard

Employed as a rollerman in Lauden during its earlier days was David Groves who had been born in Cadle near Swansea in 1820. Like many of his generation, he had initially gone to Pennsylvania and in his case, to a place that bore the very distinctive Welsh name of Cwmbwrla. Soon after his arrival he started to drift from one place to another, first to Baltimore and then on to Richmond. On his return to Pennsylvania, and after a short stay in both Bellefonte and Philadelphia, he took to his travels again, this time boarding a ship in New York that would take him as far south as Charleston, South Carolina. From there he worked his way inland through Georgia where he spent some time before continuing northward to reach Covington, Kentucky, a town located just across the Ohio River from Cincinnati. Somewhat later, and having gone to New Orleans in the meantime, he became a victim of the rumours concerning the gold that could supposedly be found in its abundance in California. There he would spend the next twenty months before visiting Covington once again and where he was offered the opportunity of working in Lauden.

After another brief journey at the outbreak of the Civil War he returned to Lauden but soon found that the circumstances were no longer to his liking. His only option was to start walking northward towards Lexington, Kentucky, a distance approaching two hundred miles. On the way he made a point of visiting the less than thriving farming community at Brynyffynnon in Scott County. Faced with having to evade Confederate soldiers, he was accompanied over part of the onward journey by one of the settlers, Cadwgan Fardd (Cadwgan the Bard). Once beyond the soldiers' reach, David Groves continued on his own until he finally reached Ironton, Ohio. However, he never lost his desire to return to Tennessee and once the circumstances would allow it, he spent a brief period in Chattanooga before eventually settling in Knoxville. He was still residing there towards the end of the century and, despite the success enjoyed by many of the city's Welsh over the intervening years, he was considered to be as prosperous as any of them.

Cadwgan Fardd would also accompany Samuel Roberts over part of his journey when he set out to visit a number of the more northern Welsh settlements in August 1863. Going as far as Cincinnati, he sought temporary employment while Samuel Roberts continued northwards and, during their absence, most of their farm crops were seized by the Union Army. Though denied proper compensation, Samuel Roberts' sister-in-law managed to sell $15 worth of butter and was paid in full for it by General Burnside himself. Samuel Roberts and Cadwgan Fardd did not return until January 1864 and among the items they were requested to bring back was some powder and shots for shooting squirrels. While it was customary to eat wild rabbits in Wales, consuming squirrel meat seems to be a novelty they had picked up from their new-found neighbours in Tennessee.

A year on, Samuel Roberts undertook another extended visit to a number of Welsh communities in the northern states. This he did despite realizing that there had been "as much deliberation over me amongst many of the Welsh as of Jeff Davies himself and that the odd Welshman in the drive for humanitarianism would have welcomed the opportunity of shooting me, for the sake of Freedom and the Union" [bod cymaint o drin wedi bod arnaf ymysg llawer o'r Cymry ag a fu o drin Jeff Davies ei hun ac y buasai ambell Gymro yng ngwres ei ddyngarwch yn hoffi cael y cyfle i'm saethu, er gwasanaeth i achos Rhyddid ac Undeb]. During his absence Cadwgan Fardd remained at his Ty'nygelli home and in a letter sent to Samuel Roberts he reveals a rather unsuspected, but sentimental side, to his character:

Ond och!!! Mr. Roberts annwyl mae Tom wedi trigo, ydyw, y mae wedi trigo; un o'r ceffylau addfwynaf tan y nef. Yr oedd gennyf fwy o olwg arno na chred yr un dyn byw. Ni theimlais hanner cymaint ar ôl yr un creadur erioed o'r blaen, ac y mae yn golled ofnadwy i mi, fel nas gwn yn y byd mawr beth a wnaf ar ei ôl. Nid oes neb yma yn gwybod beth oedd yr achos iddo drigo. Bum i ag ef yn y felin dydd Iau, 8fed o'r mis hwn, ac yr oedd mor fywiog ag y gwelsoch ef erioed. Nos Wener, y 9fed, aethum i'w weled fel arfer cyn myned i'r gwely, ond gomeddodd fwyta y corn a roddais iddo. Gelwais Beca i'w weled, a phan oeddym yn myned i'r ystabl, yr oedd yn gweryru fel pe yn ceisio dymuno arnom i leddfu ei boen; ond druan o Tom, efe a fu farw mewn ychydig fynudau. Yr wyf byth er hynny fel dyn wedi hanner hurtio, heb wybod beth i'w wneud. Mi godais ystabl dda i Tom fel y gwyddoch, ac yr oedd Tom yn ei llanw yn iawn, ond yn awr nid yw hi ond ystabl wag.

[But oh! dear Mr Roberts, Tom has died, yes, he has died; one of the most gentle spirited horses this side of heaven. I thought more of him than anybody can believe. I never felt as much after a single creature before and it's been such a tremendous loss that I don't know how on earth I can manage without him. Nobody here knows what caused his death. I took him to the mill on Thursday, the 8th of this month, and he was as lively as you ever saw him. Friday night, the 9th, I went to see him as usual before going to bed, but he refused to eat the corn I gave him. I called Beca to see him, and as we entered the stable, he was neighing as if to beg us to soothe his pain; but poor Tom, he died within a few minutes. Ever since I've been as a half-dazed man, and at a loss at knowing what to do. As you well know, I had built Tom a fine stable, and Tom filled it in a fine manner, but now it is but an empty stable.]

CHAPTER 3

Opportunities after the War

Knoxville and Coal Creek

From the eastern part of Pennsylvania where the majority of the Welsh industrial workers were located, it required an arduous journey of 650 miles to reach Knoxville in eastern Tennessee. While the countryside becomes mountainous on approaching this part of the state, it does not remain so on travelling onward for another good 400 miles to reach the state's western extreme at Memphis. On approaching this city, which lies on the Mississippi, the terrain becomes more even and it was here that the old plantations could be found and where the slaves once attended to the cotton fields. Rarely were they seen working the more hilly eastern parts and as to Knoxville itself, the Welsh would take great pride in the fact that in common with Italy's (Eidal) ancient Rome (Rhufain), it also stood on seven hills (saith bryn):

> Roedd dinas chwech yr Eidal,
> Yn sefyll ar saith bryn,
> A thebyg ydyw Knoxville,
> I Rufain fawr yn hyn.

The earliest report regarding their arrival in Knoxville appears to be the one found in the March 1868 issue of *Y Cenhadwr Americanaidd* [The American Missionary] and singled out as the first of the arrivals was Joseph Richards:

Wedi iddo ymadael o Harrisburg, hwyliodd ei gerddediad i'r
deau-orllewin, gan adael golygfeydd hyfryd, a gerddi per-lysiau,
hen dalaith Pennsylfania, a sefydlodd yn Knoxville, ym mhlith
meibion Ham. Nid oedd yma yr adeg honno, un Cymro na
Chymraes.

[*After leaving Harrisburg he directed his walk in a south-west direction,
leaving behind the splendid views and the appetizing vegetable
gardens of the old state of Pennsylvania, and settled in Knoxville,
Tennessee amongst the sons of Ham. At the time there was not a single
Welshman or woman here.*]

This had occurred in 1867 and following him later in the
year were David Richards (his brother), Daniel Thomas, J H
Jones and Daniel Jones. Their very existence would depend on
being able to get the mill that was formerly located in Lauden
to operate successfully. Given that the mill had its origins in
Danville, Pennsylvania, where some of them had previously
worked, one can safely assume that they were familiar with
whatever idiosyncrasies that it might have and which could
have hindered its use. Of greater concern would be how best
to get hold of the required raw materials and this is alluded to
in a letter written by David Richards and J H Jones. The last
named is presumably none other than the John H Jones who
had struggled with the mill in Lauden, and their joint letter
was included as part of an article that appeared in the *New York
Times* on 6 December 1868:

The undersigned, natives of Wales, having been engaged for
many years in the manufacture of iron, both in our native
country and Pennsylvania... have traced a very valuable vein of
fossilferous iron of excellent quality... 30 to 40 miles from the
city of Knoxville...

By 1868, and within a year of the first group's arrival, over a
hundred of Welsh origin had been lured to the area. According

to the Rev. Thomas Thomas, Knoxville was still suffering from the aftermath of the war and, as he himself did not arrive until 1870, one has to assume that most of his observations were based on what others had related to him. These were published in the January 1871 issue of *Y Cenhadwr Americanaidd* [The American Missionary].

Nid oedd y ddinas a'r ardal y pryd hwnnw yn ddim ond ysgerbwd truenus o wael o wehilion rhyfel. Braidd dy o fewn y ddinas yn gyfan, ugeiniau ohonynt heb yr un ffenest arnynt, ac nid oedd na llety na lluniaeth i'w gael am arian, ac y mae yn ddiddorol i wrandaw ar y fintai hon yn adrodd eu helynt.

Bu dyfodiad y Cymry i'r ddinas hon yn anadl bywyd iddi; ac mae yn dda gennyf nodi yn y fan hon fod cymeriad y Cymry fel cenedl yn uchel iawn yn y lle. Ac y mae rhai o'r trigolion yn credu fod y Cymry i gyd fel cenedl yn genedl grefyddol. (Gwyn fyd na byddai eu barn yn ffaith.) Ac mewn gwirionedd y Knoxville Iron Company a'r Machine Shop sydd yn perthyn i'r Railways ydyw bywyd y ddinas.

[*The city and its surroundings at that time was nothing but a pitiful skeleton of refuse left after the war. Hardly a house in the city in one piece, scores without a single window, and there wasn't a place to stay or food to be had for any money, and it is interesting to listen to this contingent elaborate on their predicament.*

The coming of the Welsh to this city gave it a new lease of life; and it is with pride that I note here that the character of the Welsh is held in high esteem in this place. And some of the residents believe that all the Welsh as a nation are religious. (O that their opinion was only true.) And in reality it is the Knoxville Iron Company, and the Machine Shop which belongs to the Railways, that is the life of the city.]

Even before its wartime sufferance, Knoxville had not been a particularly progressive city. In a book entitled *Knoxville, Tennessee*, William Bruce Wheeler draws attention to how this new enterprise with its manufacturing base had helped the city break away from its sleepy past:

> At the end of the Civil War, Knoxville had little that could be called industrial activity. The town could boast of only a few flour mills, small furniture shops, saddleries, foundries, and other modest enterprises… Probably the first significant manufacturing establishment in Knoxville was the Knoxville Iron Company, founded in 1867 by Hiriam S Chamberlain… Using borrowed capital, he established the Knoxville Iron Company, which by 1900 employed around 850 workers, mostly Welsh immigrants and African-Americans.

While H S Chamberlain's name is invariably associated with the company, his role appears to have been somewhat overstated. Apart from referring to Knoxville's pitiful state after the Civil War, the Rev. Thomas Thomas goes on to elaborate on Joseph Richards's initial visit to Knoxville, "The outcome was that he bought shares in the Mill, leaving a fourth part in the possession of Jones" [Y canlyniad o hynny oedd iddo brynu rhanau (shares) yn y Felin, gan adael y bedwerydd ran i Jones]. Lending credibility to the above claim regarding John H Jones's continued involvement in the mill's ownership are a few rather vague comments made by the David Groves who had once worked as a rollerman in Lauden. After acknowledging that John H Jones was not the mill's owner, he goes on to say that he had not been particularly well treated when the mill was first removed to Knoxville. Further, his belief was that the Federal Government had been slow in correcting the situation and providing him with his due reward (in a talk prepared for celebrating St David's Day, 1 March 1925 it was indicated by a later member of the Richards family that, had John H Jones remained unhindered by the war and had managed to provide iron for local use within three years, he would have been entitled to assume sole ownership of the mill). As to its post-war ownership in Knoxville, this was elaborated on in an article that appeared much later and in the 8 May 1892 issue of the weekly newspaper, *Colomen Columbia* [Columbian Dove]:

> Llwyddodd y ddau Richards a'u cyfeillion i brynu y felin. Gwnaed y cwmni hwn fyny gan mwyaf o gysylltiadau perthynasol, sef David, Joseph a William Richards, ynghyd a Daniel Thomas a Thomas Lewis. Yr oedd amryw y tu allan yn rhanddalwyr... Wedi cael pethau i ychydig drefn daeth amryw Gymry o'r gogledd i waered, a bu hyn yn fath o adfywiad i'r holl dref, yr hon oedd newydd gael ei pharlysu gan y gwrthryfel. Meddianai amryw o'r Cymry ychydig arian, a phrynasant ddarnau o dir yma a thraw er codi cartrefi iddynt eu hunain. Hwynt hwy ddechreuasant adeiladu y rhan hono o'r dref a elwir yn Mechanicsville, neu bentref y gallofyddion.

> [*The two Richards and their friends succeeded in buying the mill. This company was largely made up of acquaintances who were relatives, in David, Joseph and William Richards, together with Daniel Thomas and Thomas Lewis. There were many outsiders who were part owners... Having got a certain degree of order, many Welsh came down from the north, and in a way this served to revive the entire city, which had recently been paralysed by the war. Many of the Welsh possessed a little money, and they bought bits of land here and there for building homes for themselves. It was they who started building that part of the town called Mechanicsville, or the village of mechanics.*]

Though less detailed, essentially the same picture emerges from what was included in Goodspeed's 1887 *History of Tennessee*. From such comments as presented above it becomes apparent that the Welsh were far more heavily involved than merely contributors to the workforce as suggested in William Bruce Wheeler's book. Adding to the dominance of the Richards family was a third brother, William Richards, who had followed the initial few to Knoxville. Then married to their sister, Anne Richards, was the previously mentioned Daniel Thomas who would later oversee the running of their coal mining operation in Coal Creek. After the death of his first wife David Richards had remarried a sister to the above Thomas D Lewis who was given the responsibility of running the machine shop. In 1871 the family were left with the burden of bringing up six or seven orphaned children. This resulted from the untimely death of Daniel Thomas in December 1870 and then with the death of his wife three months later. In 1869 the company was incorporated under the name of Knoxville Iron & Coal Co. and then went on to raise $300,000 in capitalization that was needed to expand and add a foundry. On doing so it stands to reason that the family's financial interest in the company would become severely diluted.

By 1880, and through a report on the iron industry that was submitted to the Tennessee Governor by J B Killbrew, one finds that as many as 250 worked for the company and that they produced, amongst other things, up to 200 barrels of nails daily. Also mentioned in the same report was the affiliated Knoxville Foundry & Machine Shop which employed another 40. Between the two concerns they had become Knoxville's largest employer. Also indicative of their success is the fact that they were operating as many as nine puddling furnaces by the early 1880s. Still in existence near the city's centre is one of the company's original buildings, the so-called foundry which now functions as a banquet hall.

Published in the 27 June 1882 issue of *The Atlanta Constitution* is an even more informative account of the company's capabilities. By then as many as thirty nail machines were in operation, with the daily output having increased to 250 kegs. Unlike other manufacturers, they had managed to incorporate into the production process a means of discarding the five to seven pounds of defective nails that would otherwise end up in every keg. Also being produced on a daily basis was up to 40 tons of bar iron, the smallest being ⅝th of an inch wide (and presumably suitable for making horse shoes for moderately-sized ponies). Their various buildings extended over an area of two acres and alongside them all was a reservoir with a capacity to hold up to a million gallons of water.

However, not everything was as harmonious as it first appears and even prior to 1871 a group of Welsh workers, numbering from 10 to 12, had decided to branch off on their own. What became of their endeavour is not immediately apparent. Then according to a 1872 article from the *Knoxville Daily Chronicle* that dealt primarily with their religious activities, one finds that Joseph Richards had been one of twenty or so church members who had recently departed for Chattanooga. This was also alluded to in the book *Hanes Cymry America* [History of America's Welsh] which had been submitted to the press by Iorthyn Gwynedd in late 1871. In a series of Welsh-language articles from the 1890s that recalled some of their earlier exploits, there is a passing reference to David Richards as having taken over the operation of the mill in his brother's absence. The company encountered its first major setback in 1875 when it attempted to curtail the workers' wages and this led to a strike, with many leaving the area to seek temporary if not permanent employment elsewhere. Writing at the time, Iorthyn Gwynedd blamed the Welsh for "not being faithful enough to co-operate together – they brought into the company Americans from the South, relied too much on them, and at last in 1875, they got the worst of it" [ni buont yn ddigon ffyddlon i gydweithredu a'i gilydd – dygasant yr Americaniaid Deheuol i'r Company, ac ymddiriedasant ormod ynddynt, ac o'r diwedd, yn 1875, gwelsant y gwaethaf].

Close to ten years later another of their workers, a D C Richards, was to leave and organize his own company. Back in 1870 he had left the industrial centre of Dowlais in south Wales for Cleveland, Ohio and on relocating to Tennessee he had found work with the Knoxville Foundry & Machinery Co. By 1884, after 14 years with the company, he and his sons decided to branch off on their own. They went on to produce machinery for saw and grist mills which found a ready market throughout the southern states. Also having made his way to Tennessee was D C Richards's brother-in-law, the much respected Thomas Phillips who became a mining supervisor at the nearby Oliver Springs.

Not all of their endeavours were related to the iron industry and responsible for the area's first marble mill was a John D Evans who had previously operated a similar mill in Baltimore. Well known within the construction industry was R W Owens who, as an eight year-old, had been put to work at the local slate quarry in Talsarn, north Wales. His more immediate work experience had been at the Old [Slate] Quarry in Bangor, Pennsylvania and, on coming to Knoxville, he bought the construction company started by the Evan J Davies who eventually headed up a coal mining operation just over the state line in Kentucky. Such was the reputation of the construction company that when it came to utilizing slate for roofing purposes, its services were called for from as far away as Atlanta, Georgia and Selma, Alabama.

Others who succeeded beyond all expectations in Knoxville were the brothers Thomas R Price and Abram Price who ran the Knoxville Furniture Company. Having erected a large building on McGee Street in 1877, they employed between 70 and 80 workers and according to Goodspeed's *History of Tennessee*, "They obtain their material from mills on the Clinch River, and manufacture a medium grade of furniture which they sell at wholesale in all of the states east of the Mississippi and south of the Ohio." Goodspeed's history also reveals that it was Thomas R Price who was the company's president while Abram Price had taken up the position of superintendent. Given their success amongst others one can see how, by October 1892, that one of their later ministers, the Rev. Lot Lake, could proclaim: "there are in Knoxville some Welshmen who are as wealthy and content as anywhere in the country, with the Welsh Church in comfortable circumstances" [Mae yn Knoxville Gymry mor gyfoethog a chysurus ag unman yn y wlad, a'r eglwys Gymreig yn hynod o gysurus].

As to operating the iron mill itself, and being that three tons of coal are consumed in producing one ton of iron, one of their main concerns on first coming to Knoxville would have been to find a suitable supply of coal. This they accomplished through opening their own mine in Coal Creek (30 miles to the north-west) and from the previously mentioned March 1868 account in *Y Cenhadwr Americanaidd,* it appears that even at this early stage they were full of optimism about the area's coal-producing potential. Emphasized once more is the extent of their involvement in the company's overall operation:

Mae y Machine Shop a'r Foundry yn adeilad ardderchog,
ac yn eang iawn, goruchwyliwr pa un yw Thomas D Lewis,
Columbia, Pa., gynt. Hefyd, goruchwyliwr y gwaith glo yw
Daniel Thomas, Danville, Pa., gynt. Mae y glo yma yn cael ei
gydnabod gyda'r glo goreu o fewn y talaethau. Mae y wythien
hon o dair i bedair troedfedd o drwch. Wrth hyn gellir gweled
mai Cymry sydd a'r awenau yn eu dwylaw yn y lle yma, ac
nid Ellmyn na Gwyddelod chwaith. Mae y wythien uchod oll
gyda'r un Cwmni, sef Chamberlain, Richards, & Co. Fel y mae
pethau yn ymddangos yn bresenol, bydd yma lawer eto yn fuan
o'm cydgenedl…

[*The Machine Shop and Foundry is a splendid building, very
expansive, and overseen by Thomas D Lewis, formerly of Columbia,
Pa. Also in charge of the coal works is Daniel Thomas from Danville,
Pa. This coal is regarded as being the best within the States. The
vein runs from three to four feet. From this one can see that it is the
Welsh who have the reins in their hands, and not the Germans or the
Irish. All of the above vein is with one Company, viz. Chamberlain,
Richards, & Co. As things appear at present, there will be many more
of our nation here soon…*]

Ultimately as many as 150 of the Welsh would find themselves in the Coal Creek vicinity and reflecting their heritage are the surnames of the area's very first miners, viz. Eben Davis, Richard Evans, Richard Jones (Dic Bach or 'Little Dic'), Jno Jones, Tom Jenkins and Thomas Thomas. The last named would succeed Daniel Thomas as the mine's supervisor. Then within reach of the mine was a neighbourhood that had been named after the River Wye in Wales. With the opening of other mining operations such as the Coal Creek Coal Co. and the New River Coal Co., Coal Creek would be transformed from the sparsely populated area it once was to the second most populated area (after Clinton) in Anderson County. According to Goodspeed's *History of Tennessee* all this was brought about as a result "of the mining operations in that vicinity".

Not that far away from Coal Creek was Oliver Springs, now an affluent residential community. It too was once a thriving mining area and amongst those who once worked there was a Thomas J Davies whose place of birth was Llansamlet, Wales. His parents had moved to Pottsville, Pennsylvania when he was at a relatively young age and it was there and not in Wales that he had mastered the art of using the "pick and shovel". For close to 20 years he had been a superintendent to different mines in the Pottsville area and, despite his wealth of experience, he soon found that the coal and its retrieval was very different once he arrived in Oliver Springs around 1892. Nevertheless, it didn't take him long to adapt and he may even have been given some advice by the previously mentioned Thomas Phillips who had served in a similar capacity prior to his arrival.

Primarily responsible for the development of Oliver Springs, or Winter Gap as it was then called, was yet again Joseph Richards, or so it appeared to the Rev. Lot Lake who made a brief visit after first visiting Soddy in the latter part of 1882:

Mae gan Mr R [Joseph Richards] tua 2,000 o erwau o dir yn
y gymdogaeth, am yr hwn y talodd tua $30,000. Mae glo dan
llawer o'r tir, a chredir y bydd yno weithiau glo pwysig gydag
amser. Yr oedd tri pharti yn testio, neu brofi y glo yr adeg yr
oeddwn i yno, ac yr oedd tri dernyn o reilffordd yn cael eu
mesur, a bydd weithio arnynt yn fuan. Ar dir Mr R mae rhai
Sulphur Springs ardderchog. Ceir yma tua saith neu wyth math
o ddwfr bron yn ymyl ei gilydd, megys *black, white, yellow
sulphur, a magnesia chalyb*[?]. Tyn llawer yma yn ystod yr haf
er mwyn iechyd ag adloniant. Mae ganddo yma dy da, ac yn
ymyl y ffynonau; mae wedi adeiladu gwesty eang, a chlywir y
proffwydi yn dweud y bydd y ffynonau a'r gwesty yn ddigon o
ffortiwn iddo. Mae ganddo stor eang, ac y mae wedi adeiladu
amryw dai yma yn barod, y rhai y mae yn allu godi yn bur rad
gan fod ganddo ddigonedd o'r coed goreu ar ei dir, a melin lifio
gyfleus gerllaw… amcana gael sefydliad Cymreig cryf yn y lle, a
dichon nad yw yr adeg yn mhell pan y gwelir eglwys Gymreig
flodeuog yn Winter Gap.

[*Mr R [Joseph Richards] has about 2,000 acres of land in the
neighbourhood, for which he paid around $30,000. Coal is to be
had under much of it, and it is believed that over time there will be
important coal works here. When I was there three parties were at it
testing, or trying to establish the coal's presence, and three sections of
railroad were being measured, which will be worked on soon. There
are some excellent sulphur springs on Mr R's land. There are here
seven or eight sorts of water that are almost alongside each other, viz.,
black, white, yellow sulphur, a magnesia chalyb[?]. They draw many
here during the summer for health reasons and pleasure. He has a good
house, close to the wells, and has built a large hotel, and one can hear
the prophets say that the wells and the hotel will make him enough
of a fortune. He has a large store, and has built several houses here
already, which he can erect relatively cheap as he has a plentiful supply
of the best trees on his land, and a saw mill conveniently nearby… He
intends having a strong Welsh settlement in the place, and hopefully
it won't be long before one sees a flourishing Welsh Church in Winter
Gap.*]

According to a series of interviews conducted by Augusta Grove Bell for her book, *Circling Windrock Mountain*, he and his family had relocated to Oliver Springs in 1881. The railroad followed within the next two years and by 1888 he had organised the so-called Oliver Coal Company. Of his sons, Johnny would be responsible for the store which bore the name Joseph Richards & Sons, William acted as bookkeeper for the mining operation, Joseph became a mine supervisor, and Dave ran their 30-room hotel. By 1895 they had built a much larger and more prestigious hotel that ranked with the best of spa resorts. One of the stories related to Augusta Grove Bell was how, on one occasion, a foxhunt had been hurriedly arranged for the entertainment of the guests. To keep it all within sight of the more sedately seated guests on the hotel's balcony, a youngster had been tasked to drag a fox pelt around the more readily visible parts of the hotel's 500-acre estate. All would have been well had the pelt not been discarded afterwards within the hotel building and, with the hounds determined to get their just reward, it took some doing before the hotel could be emptied of its unwanted guests.

Soddy and Chattanooga

Coal Creek was by no means the only Welsh mining community that came into existence immediately after the war and, as early as January 1867, two individuals by the name of Abraham Lloyd and (Captain) J T Harris had been exploring the possibility of opening a mine in an area about 20 miles from Chattanooga. They were part of a small Welsh enterprise based in Brookfield, Ohio and while the last named was to leave after a year, he was soon replaced by a William Rees. They eventually settled on a site that was named Soddy after a so-called river that emptied itself into the Tennessee River, three miles away. This river proved to be such an obstacle that they were forced to build a bridge across it before proceeding with much else. Between that and other details – such as securing the mineral rights – two years were to go by before any coal could be extracted. Despite the initial delays, the Soddy Coal Co. would eventually employ up to 500 miners and become one of the state's foremost mining companies.

In June 1882, a correspondent from *The Atlanta Constitution* paid a visit to the mine and his detailed description on entering and observing the working conditions within the mine must have conveyed to his paper's readership the harsh realities of working underground (see appendix at the end of this chapter). By the time of his visit there were 13 miles of rail track threading through the mine, extending up to a mile and a half from the mine's entrance.

Given that there was a 300-foot drop in elevation from the mine's entrance to the coal depot, it became feasable to use an inclined gravity railroad for removing the mine's output. Located within reach of the depot were the furnaces that produced the coke which could be sold for twice as much as the coal itself. Between everything, 100,000 bushels were being shipped on a weekly basis and included amongst their buyers were nearly all of the iron manufacturers in Chattanooga. Listed as co-owners by *The Atlanta Constitution* were Abraham Lloyd, J T Williams, Lewis Morgan, J W Clitt and Colonel M H Clift. The last named was a well-known Chattanooga lawyer who was about to run for a Congressional seat at the time. In all, $300,000 had been invested in the mine and preparations were underway to add another 100 miners to the 300 employed at the time.

Ten years after the above report appeared in *The Atlanta Constitution*, another very favourable account appeared in the weeky newspaper, *Colomen Columbia*:

Mae glofa Soddy heddiw [1892] yn un o'r rhai mwyaf eang a llwyddianus yn y dalaith. Amrywia y gwythieni yma o un

trodfedd i fyny hyd bymtheg… saif y lle yn gyfleus i reilffordd
ac afon, ac anfonir glo ymaith drostynt. Y De gan mwyaf
yw eu marchnad. Mae yno 155 o ffwrnau golosg, a'r rhan
fwyaf mewn gwaith. Credir fod y lle i gynyddu llawer yn y
blynyddoedd dyfodol. Mae y cwmni yn feiddianol ar lawer o
dir. Ymestyna o Sale Creek i lawr i Daisy, pellter o tua deg
milltir, yn ymylu bob cam a llinell y Cincinnati Southern RR.,
ac ymestyna yn ôl am bellter i'r mynyddoedd. Mae eu heiddo
tirol yn werthfawr.

[*Today [1892] Soddy's coal mining is one of the largest and most
successful in the state. The [coal] veins vary from one up to fifteen
feet… the place is conveniently located within reach of the railroad
and river, and the coal is taken away on them. On the whole it is the
South that is their market. There are 155 charcoal furnaces, with most
of them in operation. It is believed that the place will expand greatly
in the coming years. Much land is in the possession of the company. It
extends from Sale Creek down to Daisy, a distance of about ten miles,
bordering all the way with the line of the Cincinnati Southern RR,
and reaching far back to the mountains. Their land holdings are very
valuable.*]

Not that distant from Soddy was the previously mentioned
Sale Creek that had provided the mill in Lauden with some of
its coal prior to the Civil War. Little was to transpire here until
another group of Welshmen decided to band together in 1867
for the purpose of developing the area. Chosen to be the mine's
superintendent was William Lloyd, a brother to the Abraham
Lloyd who was primarily responsible for Soddy's growth over the
years. One of their earlier priorities was to build a one and a half
mile long tram line so that the coal could be more readily taken
to the Tennessee River and then loaded onto barges. This mode
of transportation came to an end in 1875 when it was replaced by
the railroad. As Sale Creek's output was limited to about a fifth
of that at Soddy or Coal Creek, it never attained the same degree
of recognition.

One of the more unusual physical features of this particular area is the so-called Sunken Lake. The lake itself is a 100 feet deep and, as its surface is also a 100 feet below the encircling rock, it only occupies about three of the five-acre natural depression that occurs within the referred rock formation. Initially known as Lake Llewellyn, one can only speculate as to whether it received its original name after one of the area's early Welsh miners.

Given their relative proximity to the iron mills in Chattanooga, both Soddy and Sale Creek had a ready market for much of what they produced. Towards the end of the nineteenth century Chattanooga was regarded by many as having the potential of becoming the 'Pittsburgh of the South'. In the intervening years after the Civil War, a variety of companies such as Chattanooga Iron Co., Lookout Iron Co., Vulcan Iron Co. and Roane Iron Co. were struggling to expand their operations, with the last named being about the most noteworthy. Responsible for its financing were venture capitalists from such diverse northern states as Indiana, Ohio and New York, and despite not appearing as having any Welsh connection, they did rely on a significant number of Welshmen to fill key positions.

This company had taken its name from Roane County which lies between Knoxville and Chattanooga, and it was there that they had operated their first mill. By 1869 they had acquired the mill which the Federal Government had once used to recycle the rails sabotaged by the Confederates. This enabled them to expand into Chattanooga where they also built several puddling furnaces. Having overseen its financing was a Gen. J T Wilder from Illinois and, given that he had entered into a collaborative agreement with Col. H S Chamberlain of the Knoxville Iron & Coal Co., this may very well have been the mill which was supervised by Joseph Richards during his three-year stay in Chattanooga. If so, that would have been in the early 1870s and about a decade earlier than when many others of Welsh descent came to occupy key positions within the company. Included amongst them were the general manager, George Jones, and the puddle-boss, William Miles. The latter was to marry a daughter of the Rev. Thomas Thomas, formerly of Knoxville but who had relocated to Soddy in the meantime. Then to take care of the final straightening of the rails was an Evan Moses whose brother, the Rev. John Moses, was pastor at a Welsh-language church in Wisconsin. Between others, such as Thomas J Lewis – their chief blacksmith, at least 20 Welshmen held key positions within this company alone. All told, the company employed around 800 workers but as the demand for the iron they produced was diminishing rapidly around the mid 1880s, they were forced to start producing steel in 1886.

One Welsh visitor to the city in the early 1880s gave equal prominence to another iron producer, the Powell Iron Co. In charge of their rolling mills was a Richard Bowen whose wife was a daughter to the above mentioned Rev. John Moses of Wisconsin. An accomplished writer, his essays would often bring him prizes at the eisteddfod literary competitions. Somewhat misleading though is the visitor's claim that the company was run by a W A Powell who had left Pontypool in Wales as a five year-old in 1830. Three years later his family had relocated to Nashville where they continued to live for ten years throughout W A Powell's formative years. Yet when it came to the Civil War, it was to the Union Army that he would turn, rising through the ranks to become a general. After the war he is credited with organising the Clifton Nails Works in West Virginia (in 1867) and then a similar operation in Belleville, Illinois (in 1876). While he did visit Chattanooga in 1881, and on doing so succeeded in acquiring the Vulcan Iron & Nails Co. on his own behalf as well as two others, he would be back in Belleville, Illinois by the following year.

On closer examination one finds that this company, which was initially known as the Vulcan Iron Co., had not been a particularly thriving enterprise over the years. First started in 1860, it resumed operations after the Civil War and continued to do so until 1873 when an economic slowdown left it in financial difficulties. By 1875 it had reorganized under the name of Hazelton & Harrison. It was not until around 1880 that it became known as the Powell Iron & Nail Co., but its existence under this name barely lasted a year. Its new name of South Tredegar Iron Co. suggests that it might have become part of the well-known Tredegar Works of Richmond, Virginia. So whatever success the company experienced while operating under the name of Powell Iron & Nail Co., it was very short-lived indeed.

As with Knoxville, Chattanooga also lies on the Tennessee River but given its close proximity to Georgia and its more southerly exposure, it was more prone to having to face sudden summer storms whose destructive force was beyond the comprehension of the recently arrived Welsh. Such a storm in June 1875 alarmed one Welshman to such an extent that he sent a description of the experience to the Welsh-language newspaper, *Y Drych* [The Mirror]. Of all things he was to sign his name as Yr Hen Ŵr o Dwll y Cacwn (The Old Man from the Hornet's Nest):

> Yr oeddem oll yn achwyn ers tro ar y tywydd sych, a phawb yn dymuno am wlaw; ond oddeutu un o'r gloch y dydd a nodwyd, dechreuodd y cymylau duon grynhoi, nes oeddynt erbyn 2 o'r gloch yn edrych yn fygythiol iawn o'r gogledd-orllewin. Nid oedd un awel i'w theimlo, a'r gwres yn angherddol. Ond ar darawiad, dyma yr hen gwmwl coch bolddu hwnnw yn gollwng allan y corwynt ofnadwy – cludai bopeth o'i flaen am enyd – y tai, simneiau, a'r coedydd yn cael eu dryllio, y pridd a'r llwch yn cael ei gludo fel tonau aruthrol, nes oedd yn amhosibl gweled, na gwneud allan beth oedd yn bod; a chlywid y tan alarwm yn dechrau seinio – tybiasant hwy fod yr holl dref ar dan.

Ond dyma fellt fflamgoch yn dechrau gwau, y gwlaw a'r cenllysg yn disgyn, nes argyhoeddi pawb ar unwaith mai ystorm oedd yn myned heibio i ni, a bendigedig am hynny, myned heibio a wnaeth. Er gwneud llawer o niwed, ni chollwyd dim bywydau yma. Yn wir, golygfa ofnadwy yw bod yn llygad-dyst o frwydr elfenawl. Dyna foddion effeithiol i ymlid anffyddiaeth o'r meddwl, ie bod ynghanol ystorm – y nefoedd a'r ddaear fel wedi ymgynddeiriogi, ac yn bwgwth ei gipio ymaith bob eiliad; ac yntau'r truan i ba le y try?

[*For some time we'd all taken to complaining about the dry weather and expressing the desire for rain; but about one o'clock on the noted day, dark clouds started to gather, until by two o'clock it looked ever so threatening from the north-west. Not a single breeze was felt, and the heat had become unbearable. But at a single strike, that old black-bellied red cloud let loose the most terrible tornado – taking with it everything in its path for a brief while – houses, chimneys and trees being ripped apart, the soil and dust carried off as on a gigantic wave, making it impossible to see, or to determine what was occurring: and the fire alarm started to sound off – they being convinced that the entire city was on fire.*

But then a red flamed lightening bolt started to weave, with rain and hail coming down, and making known to all at once that it was a passing storm, and thankfully it did pass by. Though causing much damage, no lives were lost. Truly, it is a horrible sight being an eyewitness to such a mighty battle. What effective medicine for having the mind cleansed of non-belief, yes to be caught in a storm – heaven and earth aroused until irrationality prevails, and threatening to have one swept away in an instance, and the unfortunate left to wonder where should he turn?]

Despite such shortcomings, most of them seemed to be quite content with life in Tennessee. Even in Soddy, where there was not much alternative to working underground, they still regarded it as a 'braint' (privilege) to be there. Such were the sentiments expressed to the Rev. Lot Lake during his visit in 1882, and as to Wales itself, it was increasingly seen as a land of shortages and oppression. Many of the ones the Rev. Lot Lake would have met had grown up in Aberdare, a place which had experienced its own industrial expansion over the first half of the nineteenth century. During this period its non-Anglican churches had increased in number from one to sixteen, with one of them producing three pastors who eventually came to the United States (two were ministers in Michigan and Ohio and a third a faculty member at a divinity school in Delaware). In keeping with this was Aberdare's reputation of being regarded as one of Wales's leading cultural centres. Yet on the minds of many who would later make it to Soddy was how they had been depicted by Aberdare's Anglican minister in the testimony he had prepared for a 1847 government report that will be elaborated on later:

> My parish, in its present uneducated condition, is certainly retrograding… The men and the women, married as well as single, live in the same house, and sleep in the same room… The men drink in beershops… Saturday night and Monday night, and also Sunday morning are always spent drinking if the times are good. If it be after pay the carousal is generally extended till Tuesday or even Wednesday. Nothing can be more improvident than the miners or colliers… There is no religion whatever in my parish…

Jellico and Bordering Kentucky

Some fifteen years after Coal Creek had become a coal mining area, far less would be heard of its Welsh involvement. By then other opportunities had arisen some 30 miles further north in the vicinity of Jellico. This town borders onto Kentucky and within its sight, but about a mile beyond the state line, was where they started the first of their endeavours in the area. They named the place Dowlais after one of the foremost industrial centres in Wales and amongst those behind the enterprise were individuals like E J Davies, D C Richards, Moses Jones, Job Jones and William

Jenkins, all with typical Welsh surnames. Several of them had previously attempted (in 1876) to open a mine in Caryville (seven miles from Coal Creek) but to their dismay the coal vein was found to "run out here and there". This forced them back to Coal Creek and after briefly working in existing mines, they took it upon themselves to reopen a disused mine. Despite achieving success at this, they still possessed enough motivation to leave for the Jellico area in 1883.

Listed as co-owners of the Dowlais Mine in the early 1890s were E J Davies, president of the company, B A Jenkins, secretary and treasurer, D C Richards, Mrs Ruth Jenkins, D D Nicholas, W T Lewis, Mrs Margaret Leyshon and then the Phillip Francis whose expertise would be called upon during Coal Creek's horrific mining accident in 1902. Though his parents were from Caerphilly, he had been born in Pennsylvania and it was from Mahanoy City in that state that he had travelled to Dowlais in September 1883. Over the coming years he gained the respect of practically all who had come in contact with him: "a successful superintendent and worth his pay to any company. He is a sober individual, careful in his ways, and lively of spirit. He never takes the time of two steps to accomplish one" [goruchwyliwr llwyddianus, ac yn werth yr arian i unrhyw gwmni. Mae yn ddyn sobr, gofalus a bywiog ei ysbryd. Nid yw yn cymryd amser dau gam i gymryd un]. Residing with him was his father-in-law who in his earlier years had gone to California as one of the 49ers. Here, at their Dowlais, which was located in a picturesque valley, he was revered as one of their most amiable inhabitants:

> Ymddifyra yr hen frawd mewn hollti coed, cario glo, chwilio
> am y ffynhonnau gorau, tremio i'r nentydd am bysg, teithio
> y coedwigoedd, cyfrif yr adar, ac ysbio eu nythod. Mewn
> rhyw ystyr, efe yw maer y pentref. Caffed yr hen frawd dipyn
> o amser da o hyn i derfyn ei daith, a heddwch Nef pan yn
> noswylio.

[The *old brother keeps himself amused through splitting wood, carrying coal, seeking out the best wells, gazing into the creeks for fish, strolling through the woods, counting birds, and noting their nests. In one way, he is the mayor of the village. May the old brother have some good times from now to the journey's end, and the peace of Heaven when night falls.*]

Despite being located in Kentucky, the company was to become known as the East Tennessee Coal Co. Having secured the mining rights to 2,200 acres, their coal proved to be particularly suitable for domestic use and it found a ready market throughout much of the South. Their daily output of around 400 tons was reflected in the substantial profits that were said to be paid out to its shareholders. The coal yard and offices which they operated in Knoxville soon acquired the reputation of being the place to go to if one was overcome with a desire to link up with others of Welsh extraction. Back in Dowlais itself, and rather unexpectedly residing there towards the end of the century, was one of the former families of the abandoned Brynffynnon settlement. Identified as living there were a Margaret Jones, her son Robert, and daughter Lissie, but no indication is given as to their whereabouts from the time Samuel Roberts returned to Wales in 1867 until Dowlais came into existence in 1883.

Also within easy reach of Jellico was another Welsh settlement that once went by the name of Proctor. While contemporary maps of Kentucky show a so-called place about 75 miles from the Tennessee border, earlier Welsh-language accounts refer to a Proctor that was within three miles of Jellico. Also suggestive of a place so-named in such close proximity is the Proctor Road that leads out of Jellico itself. Then there is the name of the mine itself, the so-called Jellico Mining Co. Chosen to be its superintendent when first started in 1892 was the Walter S Lewis who, together with his father, had accompanied Philip Francis on his journey from Mahanoy, Pennsylvania in 1883. Already making preparations for the opening of the Dowlais mine back at the time of their first arrival was a Harry Wyn who, by now, had become the new mine's 'boss'. By the turn of the century the Proctor mine would employ around 250 miners and, given that Walter S Lewis was described as being a "thoroughly red blooded Welshman" [o waed coch cyfan], it comes as no surprise to find that the Proctor mine was generally regarded as being totally dominated by the Welsh.

Somewhat further afield, yet within six miles of Jellico, was another community that took its name after the Mountain Ash found in Wales. Like Proctor, it was also settled in 1892 and before the year was out they had managed to organize both a choir and a brass band. Chosen as the mine's president was the Evan J Davies who already served in a similar capacity at Dowlais. Located within the same mountain range but six miles further afield, was Williamsburg with its seven mines. These were said to employ around 700 miners altogether and being that the Mountain Ash Choir was rehearsing a new cantata for their entertainment over the Christmas period in 1892, it appears that this place also had a strong Welsh contingent. Then, located between Mountain Ash and Williamsburg is another place that went by the Welsh name of Emlyn, but practically nothing is known regarding its early existence.

Given the early emergence of Pittsburgh, Pennsylvania as the country's foremost industrial centre, it is not particularly surprising to find similarly named places in other states, and Kentucky was no exception. Located only half a mile away from its Pittsburgh was the Baxtertown that got its name from a Lewis Baxter who hailed from Llanidloes in Wales. Through having once worked at Ynys Hir near Porth and then in the Rhondda Valley, he was well positioned to open Baxtertown's Victoria Coal Mine. This he accomplished in the early 1880s and listed with him as co-owners were not only two sons but also two sons-in-laws. With such a family presence it is not difficult to see how the town got its name and, despite being separated by around 40 miles from the cluster of mining communities in the Jellico area, they did manage to interact socially with them. Further afield again, and situated about 50 miles east of Baxtertown, was another place called Glomawr (literally Big coal). One brief account suggests that it only came into being in 1914 and that through the efforts of the East Tennessee Coal Co.

Finally, one other place deserves a passing mention, and that in view of it having been named after the principal city in Wales. Behind the so-called Cardiff Coal & Iron Company was a group of northern investors, none of them having a particularly Welsh name. The land holdings were located 40 miles west of Knoxville and, in 1890, an attempt was made to raise an additional $5,000,000 in capitalization. On doing so they claimed that their property had not only a vein of iron ore that ran up to four feet thick but also all the necessary coal and chalk. It was anticipated that iron could be produced for around eight dollars a ton, with three dollars of it going towards the salaries of workers. Further, it was estimated that for every ton of iron produced, it would need 1.75 tons of coke, 2.75 tons of iron ore, and half a ton of chalk. Between the nearby Walden Ridge and the Tennessee River, which was less than four miles away, it had every appearance of being a very desirable place to reside in. Yet it does not feature in any Tennessee related articles that appeared from time to time in the country's Welsh-language press. A plausible reason for such a lack of interest is suggested by a court ruling that found the company at fault for not developing the town to the extent promised in its public offering. Today one has to look twice before finding Cardiff on the current road maps of Tennessee.

Overseeing Coal Creek's Boarding House

One of the more pressing issues they faced initially at Coal Creek was how best to accommodate the first of its miners. Through an obituary written in memory of a Margaret Davies, one discovers that she had been responsible for running a boarding house there from as early as April 1867. Her husband, a blacksmith named David Davies, had died in 1859, and that prior to her leaving Wales. Left under her care were not only her own five children but also the three orphaned children of her brother-in-law. Three of her own children, Thomas, Joseph and Mary eventually settled in Knoxville and so it is only natural that she should end her days there as well. Her son Thomas had his own blacksmith shop on Chamberlain Street, alongside the highly successful machine shop started by D C Richards and his sons. The daughter Mary married a Thomas T Thomas and being that her sister Elizabeth was also married to a Thomas Thomas, it probably was a blessing that he resided some distance away in Virginia. Mary Ann, an adopted daughter, married the Rev. George W Smith who was once a miner in Coal Creek, but later took up the ministry and moved to take care of a Welsh church in Soddy. Towards the end of 1869, and at the urging of her children, Margaret Davies was persuaded to give up working in Coal Creek and move to Knoxville. Over the years she became to be affectionately known as Antie Peggy.

Related to her back in Wales was her much admired cousin, the renowned Henry Richard of Tregaron. According to *Y Fellten* [The Lightning], a local weekly newspaper from Merthyr, his election to the British

Parliament in 1868 resulted in much rejoicing, not only amongst his constituents in industrial Merthyr, but throughout all of Wales:

Y mae Ymneillduwyr Merthyr, Faelor, ac Aberdar wedi codi eu hunain i'r anrhydedd uchaf drwy ethol Mr. Henry Richard i'w cynrychioli yn Senedd-dy Prydain Fawr... yr oedd Eglwyswyr wedi meddianu pob sefyllfa o ddylanwad ac uchafiaeth drwy ein gwlad am ganoedd o flynyddau... Drwy yr etholiad hwn mae Cymru wedi cyrraedd safle uwch nag un a gyrhaeddodd hi er pan y concwerwyd hi gan y Saeson... Y mae efe yn aelod, nid yn unig dros Ferthyr, ond dros holl Gymru.

[*The Dissenters of Merthyr, Faelor, and Aberdare have uplifted themselves to the highest honour by electing Mr Henry Richard to represent them in Great Britain's Parliament... the Anglicans had taken hold of every situation of influence and importance throughout our country for hundreds of years... through this election Wales has achieved a higher status than it ever had since being conquered by the English... He is a member, not only for Merthyr, but for all of Wales.*]

The paper's enthuisiastic support was later justified when he used his new-found status to become one of the leading advocates for forming the League of Nations, the forerunner of the United Nations. Despite all the hardships that Margaret Davies had endured while raising eight children on her own, it appears that she had also been blessed with some of the traits of her illustrious cousin. The verse below, which dates from the time of her death at the age of 72 in 1882, expresses the sentiment of how she too deserved to be remembered alongside those pious women (dduwiol ferch) of impeccable character and charm (llawn o serch) that were once so prevalent in Wales itself:

Yn ei plith saif Marg'ret Davies,
(Modryb Peggy) dduwiol ferch,
Oedd i lu yn adnabyddus
Fel gwraig bur a llawn o serch…

Special Correspondence of *The [Atlanta] Constitution*

Soddy Coal Mines, Tennessee, 15 June [1882]

At ten o'clock this morning under the guidance of Mr A[braham] Lloyd, the superintendent, and also one of the owners, I entered the mines, the first I had ever explored… Having donned a regulation mining suit, our party… took a seat in a small car about two and a half feet wide and four feet long. I say took a seat – I don't mean that – we squatted. There was no place to sit except on the floor of the car. A mule drew the train, there being two other cars, and in a minute or so we were going, it seemed to me, at the rate of ten miles an hour. At the entrance the tunnel is seven or eight feet high, but about a hundred yards under it grows beautifully less, until one is warned not to put any fingers outside the edges of the car and to keep the head as low as possible…

"How high are these tunnels?" I asked Mr Lloyd when he had cautioned us about keeping our heads low.

"They vary from three foot eight inches to four and a half feet."

"You don't mean to say these mules go through a hole only three feet eight inches high, do you?"

"Yes I do. They have a way of stooping, and can run their level best without even touching a hair on their backs."

When we had gone about half a mile the car stopped and Mr Lloyd invited us to get out. Proceeding down a branch tunnel afoot for a hundred yards or more, we came to a brace of sturdy miners digging away in a 'room' as it is called… Having crawled into the room which was only about two feet and a half high, we watched the miners dig until our necks were absolutely stiff from bending. Cramming a man into a den like that seemed horrible enough, even for a brief visit, but to contemplate spending ten years of ones life in such a position was worse than horrible…

But the life! I took the pick from a miner named Roberts and tried to dig. I am stronger than the average miner, but it seemed like cutting through flint. So far as digging coal is concerned I am a miserable failure. The miner took the pick and, in a few minutes, had gone two or three inches under the bottom of the vein. To make the work all the more horrible, they only dig right on the bottom of the vein, this being done in order to prevent making fine coal. When the pick can't go any further, a hole is drilled and a blast of powder put in the fuse and lighted. A pound of powder often brings out lumps weighing several tons, and thus a great deal of labour is saved. When the fuse is touched off, the miner runs or crawls behind a ledge or corner a few feet away until the explosion occurs. These explosions can be heard in every part of the mine, and felt like a shock of an earthquake, the concussion being very strong and hard. In Roberts' room, a blast had just been made, and the foul air from the powder was almost unbearable. But they don't seem to mind it much.

"I have three boys and we together earn five dollars and a half a day."

"So you like to dig coal?"

"Like it, sir? Why, I could not be happy at anything else."

CHAPTER 4

Conflicts and Disasters

Convict Labour

As a result of all the uncertainties throughout the southern states after the Civil War, unemployment was rampant and just about every commodity was in short supply. Without a ready means of earning a livelihood, it's hardly surprising that the state penitentiary in Nashville had reached its saturation point, with more inmates than could be readily accommodated. In an attempt to curtail the cost of sustaining such an institution, a law was passed in 1871 that led to the use of convict labour in the mines. When confronted by a strike in 1875, the Knoxville Iron Co. had a ready-made excuse for their introduction into Coal Creek's original mine. This came about despite David Richards's strong objection, his belief being that convict labour should be confined to building and maintaining state highways. Though this particular mine has long been abandoned, it still bears the stigma of being referred to as the Convict Mine.

The extent of such practices can be gauged from a report prepared by officials of the State Penitentiary that was included as part of an appendix attached to the *House Journal of the Forty-Fourth General Assembly of the State of Tennessee* (first session, 1885). It shows that a majority of those sentenced to serve time were placed under the care of mining companies. Confined at the main prison was a total of 528, but another 774 could be found distributed between Tracy City (436), Inman (177) and Coal Creek (161). The report goes on to state that:

> Tracy City is headquarters for the Tennessee Coal, Iron,
> & Railroad Company, who are the present lessees of the
> Penitentiary. They work and control sixty per cent of the
> entire prison force, and sub-lease the remainder (including all
> mechanics) to Cherry, Morrow & Co.

It is worth noting that, as Soddy does not figure in the above report, it appears that they had managed to avoid the use of convict labour altogether. However their presence in Coal Creek caused many of its Welsh to seek work elsewhere and, as a consequence, their early domination of the area came to an end. Years later, and in its 15 July 1891 issue, the *Knoxville Journal* would recall how their editor had witnessed the forlorn look on their faces as the convicts started to arrive:

> Years ago, the editor of the Journal went on the train that
> carried the first shipment of convicts to any East Tennessee
> mine. The memory of that night's ride, the manacled felons,
> the slow cautious running of the train, the frequent stops to
> inspect vulnerable points on the road and above all the neat
> cottages of the miners at Coal Creek, still lingers in his mind.
> And the difference between the cheery homes that bright
> morning, with their snowy curtains and bright-hued flowers
> in the yards, and the hopeless, desperate look to be seen on
> the faces of the thrifty Welsh miners whose places in the mines
> were being filled by the scum of the earth, will always be
> present in his memory.

Writing from Washington in 1882, a M Llewelyn would recall how he had spent 7½ years in Coal Creek "superintending the works of the Knoxville Iron Company until forced away by the introduction into the mines of that great curse – convict labour". A brief account dating from 1885 which appeared in the Welsh-orientated magazine *The Cambrian* refered to the unfortunate circumstances that they were left to confront:

The mines were owned and operated at first, almost
exclusively, by the Welsh people, but since the ownership has
past into other hands, the Welsh miners and all free labour
has been almost entirely displaced by that present curse on
Tennessee – the convict labour system, which as far as it goes,
is worse than the former slavery curse.

Not all were to leave Coal Creek but the above *Cambrian*
account goes on to imply that the number remaining barely
exceeded the eleven families they went on to identify. As some of
these names reoccur elsewhere, they are worth noting: 1. Dr Levi
Jones Price, 2. John Morgan, 3. Richard Jones (former resident of
Chattanooga), 4. James George (Cornish but married to daughter
of Wm Llywelyn in Knoxville), 5. John Jenkins (engineer from
Aberdare), 6. R M Chapman (married to another daughter of
Wm Llywelyn in Knoxville), 7. William Jones (miner from
Glynneath), 8. David D Jones (mine owner from Cydweli), 9.
Ebenezer Davies, 10. Rees R Thomas, 11. David R Thomas.

Towards the end of the 1880s one hears once more of how
"Some of the Welsh have remained in the place, with many in
comfortable circumstances. Still there to this hour the old brother
John Morgan (Bishop Morgan)..." [Y mae rhai Cymry wedi aros
yn y lle ac y maent, rai ohonynt, mewn amgylchiadau cysurus.
Yno mae yr hen frawd John Morgan (Esgob Morgan) yn aros hyd
yr awr hon...]. Any such mention of a Bishop Morgan brings
to mind the much revered sixteenth-century translator of the
Welsh Bible and implied here, therefore, is someone of a pious
nature. Consequently, it comes as no surprise to find that he was a
much admired deacon at the Coal Creek church before it stopped
functioning. Generally considered to be Coal Creek's very first
resident, he eventually left when both he and one of his sons
relocated to Rockhold, Kentucky. This occured in 1908, a few
years prior to his death at the age of 81. An obituary from the
period reveals that he had lost a limb while serving with the Union

Army during the Civil War. Also to be found in Coal Creek when a Thomas J Davis died in 1909 were his two daughters and their families. The effect of having to live with convicts in their midst proved to be almost as devastating as the loss or curtailment of wages. Their experience in Coal Creek serves to illustrate how disruptive any such unwelcome outside influence can be on what was once a vibrant community:

> Dywedir fod llawer o Gymry yn gweithio yn y gweithfeydd cyfagos yn bresennol, ond nad ydynt yn mynychu un math o addoliad, na byth yn cyfarfod yn gymdeithasol. Peth difrifol yw byw a chodi plant ym machellau anghysbell y mynyddau yma. Mae penydion wedi bod yn gweithio yma, mewn un lofa, am tua 15 mlynedd, ac mae eu bodolaeth hwy wedi bod yn ddiraddiad i'r lle ym mhob ystyr.

> [*It is said that many of the Welsh are employed in the neighbouring mines at present, but they never frequent any form of religious service, nor ever meet socially. It is a terrible thing to live and raise children in the remote nooks of these mountains. The convicts have worked here, in one mine for about 15 years, and their very presence has had a degrading influence on the place.*]

About the only positive thing to emerge from their presence was the introduction of a new word into the Welsh language that is unique to Tennessee. From the word *penyd*, which is usually associated with those undertaking religious penance in the Middle Ages, they coined the word *penydion* for those confined to the penitentiary. What transpired in Coal Creek over a century ago bears a striking resemblance to what is presently occuring to traditional communities in many parts of Wales. Left at the mercy of an overwhelming number of outsiders who show very little inclination of becoming part of the local culture and attaining proficiency in the language, one community after another is being stripped of its former well-being. It is nothing short of ethnic oppression at its non-violent worse – and that in a country that once, through its Arthurian related legends, had done as much as any country to foster a European-wide literary tradition.

Though such a misuse of convicts came to be acceptable through much of the South, by the 1890s the situation had become completely intolerable to the miners in the Coal Creek area itself. Their stance was triggered by an attempt, on the part of the Tennessee Coal Co., to introduce convicts into another mine located about four miles away at a more recently developed area called Briceville. Though it had only come into existence in 1888, a dispute had already arisen by 1891. Under contention were a number of issues, ranging from the miners desire to have outsiders weigh the coal, to their objection over being paid with the company's scrip money. Then there was the company's insistence that the miners continue to work whatever their grievance. As early as 1871 the same company had made an agreement with the State of Tennessee to have 100 convicts work at another mine. The person responsible for their introduction into the company's Briceville mine in 1891 was the American-born A Jenkins. Of Welsh extraction he is, in all likelihood, the person referred to with such utter contempt in one Welsh-language report that the writer refused to 'dignify' him through revealing his name.

The trouble started when 40 convicts were sent in advance to construct a stockade for their confinement. This occurred on 5 July 1891 and, after the stockade's completion, the expectation was to have the main convict contingent transported there on 15 July. However, on the prior evening and without any advance warning to the authorities, the so-called free miners took it upon themselves to make those first 40 convicts walk to Coal Creek and then have them board a Knoxville-bound train. As could be expected, such an insurrection on the part of the miners couldn't be tolerated by Tennessee's Governor and he was left with no alternative but to adhere to the original arrangement and order the convicts back to Briceville.

Not to be outdone, and having armed themselves with whatever guns they could find in the meantime, around 2,000 miners converged on Briceville on 21 July. The full complement of a 150 convicts were then force-marched to Coal Creek and once in the vicinity of the Knoxville Iron Co. mine, the free miners split in two. This was done in order to initiate the release of that mine's convicts as well. All were duly placed on a train heading for Knoxvile and according to the 21 and 22 July issues of the *Washington Post,* the miners showed considerable restraint and received the support of other miners further afield:

> 21 July – At 10 o'clock this morning 2,000 miners, farmers, and other natives who had no occupation at all, took possession of the hills around Briceville camp. Fifteen hundred of these were armed with rifles, the rest with shotguns and pistols. They came from all the mines in a radius of 50 miles… The miners are under almost military discipline, are sober, and no whisky is allowed in their line.

> 22 July – A telegram was received from the Kentucky side at Jellico today, offering a large number of men in case help was needed… Nearly every man present had a double-barreled shotgun in his hand, a few Winchesters, and not a small number of revolvers.

After considerable deliberation involving the State Governor, it was decided to have the convicts returned and back working at the two mines by 25 July. Despite the miners' rather undignified reference to the soldiers accompanying the convicts as "spider-legged, cigarette smoking dudes", every precaution was taken to ensure that no harm should come their way. In the meantime, a deputation of miners was sent to Nashville to plead their case with the state government, but no resolution was forthcoming. As a result, the 163 newly-placed convicts at the Tennessee Coal Mine in Briceville and the 120 long-serving convicts at the Knoxville Iron Co. mine were set free on 31 October. On 2 November they were joined by an additional 200 from a third location in Oliver Springs. This time the free miners went a step further by setting all the released convicts loose to roam the countryside at will. Headlines such as provided by the *New York Times* would have provoked the attention of even the most casual of readers:

> NEARLY FIVE HUNDRED CRIMINALS LOOSE IN TENNESSEE AND KENTUCKY.
>
> MORE CONVICTS RELEASED: THE MINERS LIBERATE THE MEN AT OLIVER SPRINGS.
>
> THEY BURN THE STOCKADE, HOSPITAL, AND OTHER BUILDINGS.

Included amongst what was burnt was the stockade at Briceville, but the one at Coal Creek was spared – apparently at the request of the convicts themselves. Attached to it was the home of the manager and, according to one account, the released convicts pleaded that the wife of the manager, who was described as "gentle and kind Welsh woman [should] not be frightened or put in danger". Despite the destruction of the other two stockades, the convicts would be back by the last day of 1891 with 880 state militia posted on a hill overlooking the Knoxville Iron Co. mine. Still to be seen on the so-called Militia Hill are the earthworks dug to their detriment by the convicts themselves.

At a mass gathering in Knoxville, Henry R. Gibson, the university chancellor, went as far as to pay tribute to the miners: "In all likelihood the world has never seen so much forebearance as these miners have exercised under so great a provocation." With the miners vowing not to give in, the Governor eventually lost all credibility and another was elected in his place. As a result of the miners continued opposition, the law was eventually changed and in 1895 it became illegal to forcefully use convicts in the mines. As a consequence, the State of Tennessee was burdened with the extra cost of having to build two additional penitentiaries.

As detrimental as the convict presence had been on the Coal Creek community, it paled in comparison to what the convicts themselves had to endure. The following account which appeared in the *Washington Post* on 25 September 1887 provides one example of how their safety had been jeopardized over the years:

> A mutiny of convicts is reported at the Knoxville Iron Company's mine at Coal Creek. They refused to go to the mine yesterday afternoon and the guard opened fire on them, wounding three or four; one is thought to be mortally wounded. The cause of the trouble is said to have been the refusal of the superintendent to move the coal away from the mouth of the pit, thus preventing free circulation of air.

They also faced the possibility of being flogged, particularly when their output fell below expectation. Many would not outlive their sentences and, in a manner reminiscent of how once in Wales one could be exiled to Australia for such trivial reasons as the theft of enough cheese to alleviate hunger, the southern courts would likewise pronounce unjustified sentences whenever a shortage of labour arose in the mines. Yet, to its credit, Tennessee became the first southern state to prohibit forced labour in the mines. By contrast, such abusive practices prevailed in Alabama until 1910. In one television documentary that dealt with the historical background of the so-called chain gangs, the local miners of Coal Creek were singled out for their heroic efforts: The free miners of Coal Creek are credited with abolishing the convict lease system in the South, an institution that was worse than slavery...

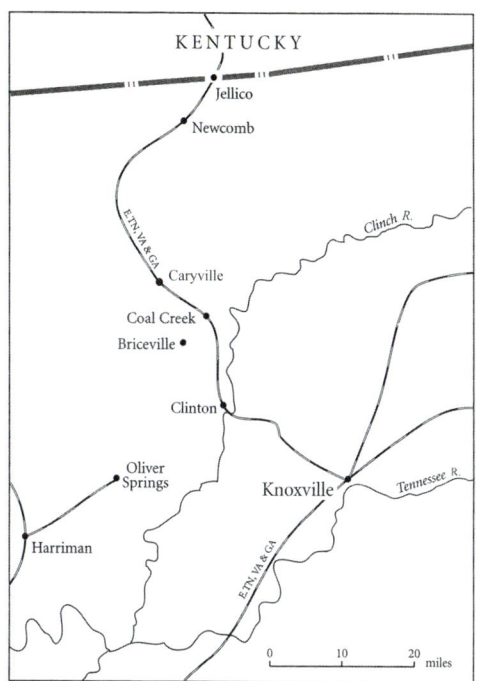

1. Map showing places of interest in the vicinity of Knoxville. (Adapted from *Hudson's Coal Miners' Insurrection 1891–1892*)

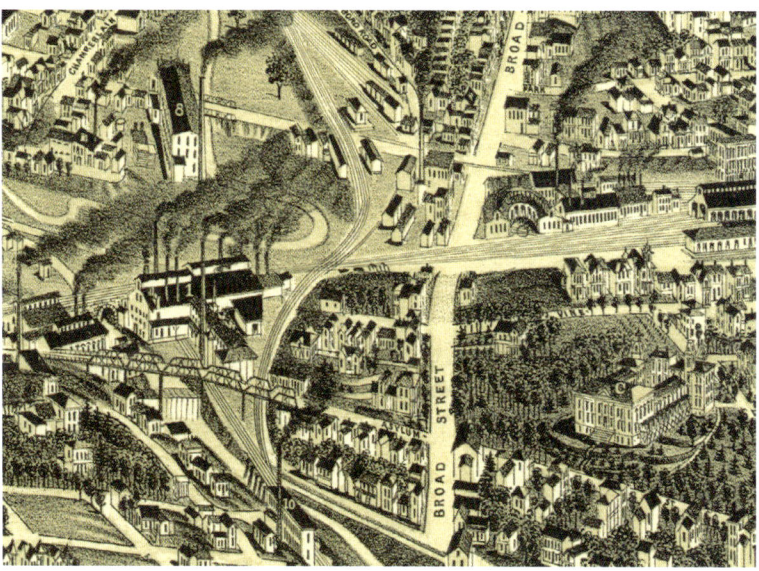

2. Industrial part of Knoxville as depicted in 1886. The most striking building immediately behind the cluster of Knoxville Iron's chimney stacks, and marked with the figure 8 on its roof, is that of the Price brothers' furniture company. (Library of Congress LC Panoramic Map 900)

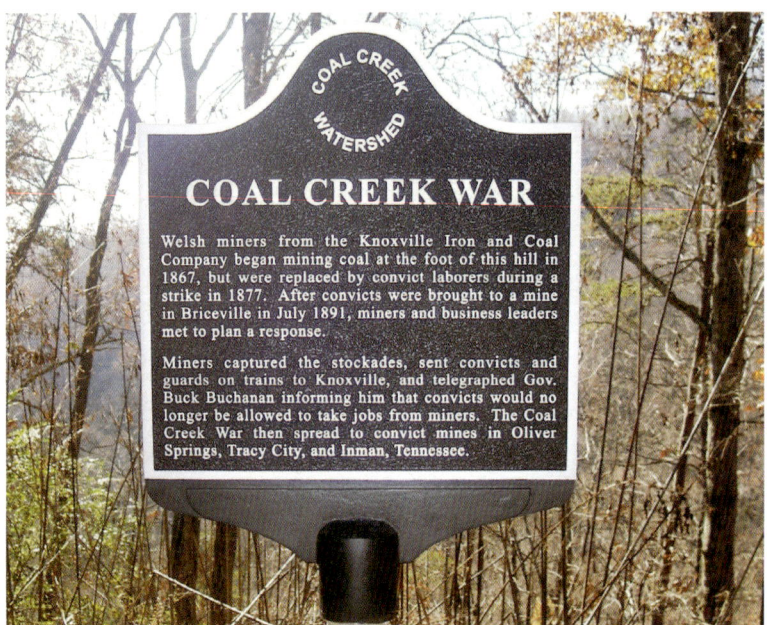

3. Coal Creek War historic marker. (Photograph courtesy of Coal Creek Watershed Foundation)

4. Meeting up with the Tennessee Governor during the Coal Creek War. David R Thomas can be seen immediately in front of the tree and wearing a bowler hat. (Photograph taken by McCrary and Branson for *Harper's Weekly*)

5. Briceville Church as it appears today. (Photograph courtesy of Coal Creek Watershed Foundation)

6. Robert McGinnis and the author attempting to decipher an eroded
    inscription towards the base of Iorthyn Gwynedd's headstone. (Photograph
    courtesy of Billy MacNamara)

YR ANRH. DAVID RICHARDS, KNØXVILLE, TENN.

7. Two of Knoxville's community leaders – Iorthyn Gwynedd and David
    Richards. (Taken from *Y Cenhadwr Americanaidd* and *Colomen Columbia*)

8. Chattanooga area in 1863 with Union soldiers crossing the Tennessee River by a pontoon bridge. (Alfred H Guernsey, *Harper's Pictorial History of the Civil War*, 1866)

9. The fallen headstone of Rees Thomas. (Photograph courtesy of Coal Creek Watershed Foundation)

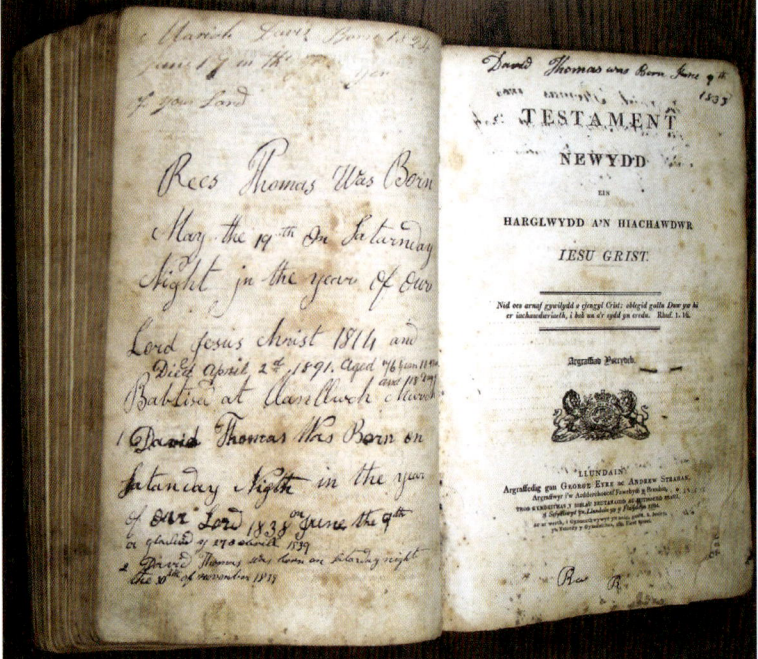

10. The family Bible of Rees Thomas. (Photograph courtesy of Coal Creek Watershed Foundation)

11.   One of the roads leading into Glomawr, Kentucky. (Photograph courtesy of
Coal Creek Watershed Foundation)

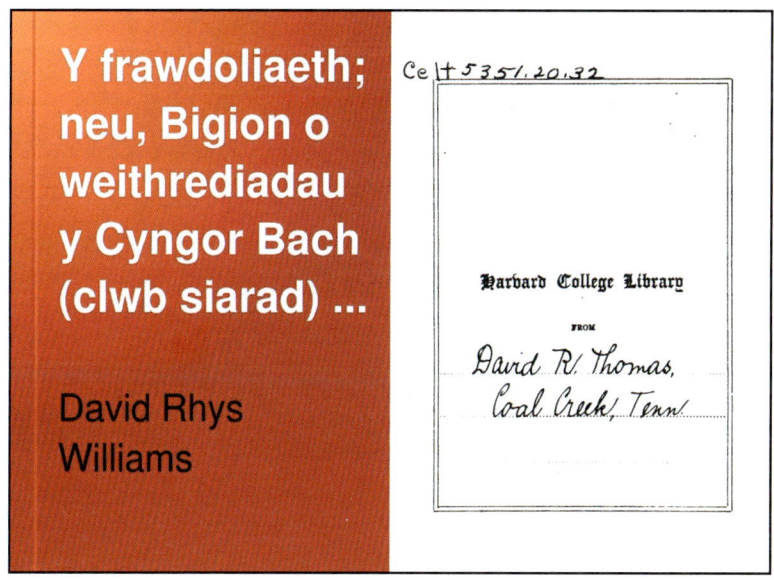

12.   One of the many books donated to Harvard University by David R Thomas.

13. A painting showing Knoxville Iron's facilities, obtained from Kathryn M Brown.

Mining Disasters

While the miners of Oliver Springs were very much involved in the confrontation over the use of convict labour, they were fortunate enough to escape the mining disasters that befell the Coal Creek area at the very beginning of the twentieth century. On 19 May 1902, an early morning explosion claimed the life of every miner present at the nearby Fraterville Mine:

> It was on one Monday morning,
>   On the nineteenth of May;
> Near two hundred miners round us,
>   Left their home and marched away…

Before the full extent of the disaster was realized, they had sought the help of the aforementioned Philip Francis from the Dowlais Mine. As the explosion had been forceful enough to strip the coal carts of their wheels, it was immediately apparent to one of his experience what lay ahead:

> … they wired me to come at once and to bring experienced miners with me… Men, women, and children were crying at the entrance of the mine. It was heart-rendering to hear them.
>
> I had charge of several men. I told them that there could not be a living miner in the mine and that we should go carefully and not get into foul air, and that I would go in front. I knew the effects of 'black damp' and 'white damp'. There comes a shortness of breath and a feeling of weakness in the knees and elbows and stillness. In that state, you must gather up all your willpower to know where you are and what you are doing and not turn yourself around too quickly, or you may fall down and lose consciousness. In one damp, your light will not burn while in another damp, it burns and both are dangerous to life. No open lights were allowed in the rescue party. I carried my own safety lamp, but it gave a very poor light. The mine had penetrated into the mountain for nearly three miles at this time and I could not travel the main entry but by byways and

airways, and then had to travel in a stooping position. The height was less than four feet. This made travelling tiresome. Some of the men had no light, but followed along the best they could. Some were uneasy when told on the outside of the mine that some fire may be left in the old workings and that a second explosion may take place.

... On the inside, you must forget the cries of women and children and also forget many dangers that surround you in the mine. You have a duty to perform to a fellow miner and to remove dead bodies to their relatives on the outside.

According to one report from the period, "only one man escaped instant death and he was blown out of the entrance of the mine by the force of the explosion." In his sixties, and having survived mining disasters in both Wales and Pennsylvania, he had the misfortune of walking by the mine's entrance at the very instance the explosion occurred. The severity of the explosion could be gauged by the way one of his eyes had been torn from its socket, and even he succumbed to his injures within three days. Three days were also to go by before all of the bodies could be retrieved and the agonizing of the women who had up to then refused to give up all hope, was recently portrayed by the 2004 production of the play *Measured in Labour*.

The initial intent was to bury the remains of those lost at the nearby Leach Cemetery but, as an objection arose over the inclusion of blacks, less than half were eventually laid to rest there. Their headstones, set out in two large concentric circles around a central memorial, are more reminiscent of the druidic stone circles of Wales than what is considered a typical cemetery layout. Another three-dozen miners were buried on the far side of Coal Creek at the Longfield Cemetery. As most of the Welsh had long left the area, relatively few Welsh surnames appear amongst the dead – four Evanses, two Robertses, one Price and one Morgan and then the Tommy

Davies whose relatives still reside in the Knoxville area. As to the eleven African-Americans who lost their lives, eight were eventually buried in the Welsh cemetery, which, by now, is almost totally obscured by the thick overgrowth on a nearby mountain side. Such a degree of tolerance on their part is not totally unexpected when one considers a comment which was to appear in *Y Drych* [The Mirror] in the early 1890s. It shows willingness on their part to share deep-felt religious experiences with African-Americans:

> Clywais rai yn dweud y fan a'r lle, a'r awr a'r funud y'u ganwyd mewn ystyr ysbrydol, yr adeg y cynyrchwyd ynddynt obaith bywyd gwell... Clywais Negroes yn Coal Creek, Tenn., yn cyfaddef, mewn dagrau... iddi golli ei chrefydd yn y fan a'r fan, ond gorfoleddai iddi wrth fynd heibio y lle mewn wythnosau ar ôl hynny gael gafael arni.

> [*I've heard some relate as to the place and spot, the hour and even the minute when they were born in a spiritual way, that instant of time when they experienced that hope for a better existence... I heard a Negress in Coal Creek, Tenn., confess, in tears... how she'd lost her faith in such and such a place, but how she'd rejoiced on going by the spot after some weeks and regaining all that had been lost.*]

While relatively few African-Americans were employed at this particular mine, many more managed to find employment when it came to the iron mills themselves. A substanial number worked at the mills in both Knoxville and Chattanooga and, while other workers were tolerant of their presence to some degree, this goodwill quickly disappeared when they started to compete for higher paid skilled positions (see the 1941 book, *The Negro in Tennessee, 1865–1880* by A A Taylor of Fisk University). However, an article from *The Atlanta Constitution* in 1882 noted that not all African-Americans were confined to performing the more menial tasks at the Knoxville Iron Company: "They use what can only be found in one other place in America, viz.: Black

Puddlers. They find that colored puddlers do about as well as any other kind. A mill in Pittsburgh also uses black puddlers."

One of those to testify as to the cause of the explosion which had taken the lives of eleven African-Americans, amongst others, was a William M Lewis, aged 49, who was employed as a mine foreman in LaFollette, Tennessee. While participating in the rescue attempt he had observed an opening between the Fraterville Mine and recently abandoned Knoxville Iron Company Mine:

> I have had 18 years experience in mines, 3 years as a fire boss in south Wales, 15 years as a miner and mine foreman in the United States, in Kentucky, Colorado, Iowa, Virginia and Tennessee... In my opinion, the furnace [for air extraction] had not been running Saturday night or Sunday and possibly was not fired until Monday morning, that gas collected in the Fraterville Mine from the old workings or that possibly they had a fall in the old Knoxville Iron Company Mine, which forced the fire damp into the Fraterville Mine...

While accidents of such a magnitude were rare, life-threatening injuries were a common occurrence. In May 1886, a rather unusual accident occurred near the Soddy Mine and, as was often the case, it was brought about by carelessness on the part of those involved. One of the more detailed accounts of what had transpired appeared in *The Atlantic Constitution*:

> Further details of the terrible explosion of 100 kegs of [blasting] powder near the Soddy coal mines, yesterday afternoon, have been received tonight. One of the engines of the company was going from the railroad station to the mine with the powder in charge of Will Loyd and Dave Harper. The engine was running at a furious rate, when a keg of powder was overturned and the contents scattered in the car. The next moment a spark from the engine ignited the powder and a terrible explosion followed. Three seconds after the spark fell, every keg of

the powder had exploded, and three bodies lay fifty feet
away down an embankment. The effect of the exposion was
frightful. The engine and two flat cars were torn to atoms, and
some portions of these were hurled a hundred yards. When the
explosion occured a miner named Ramsey was standing near
the track waiting for the train to pass. He, together with Lloyd
and Harper, were thrown down the embankment, and when
found all were in a dying condition…

Whatever were the lesser accidents they had to endure in
the Coal Creek area over the years, they would be completely
overshadowed by the horrendous loss of life, not only at the
Fraterville Mine in 1902, but by yet another accident of almost
the same magnitude nine years later. The latter took place at
the Cross Mountain Mine in Briceville on 9 December 1911
and an account in the *New York Times* the following morning
pronounced that "between 126 and 156 men are entombed here
tonight in the Great Cross Mine of the Knoxville Iron Company".
Many of the miners would travel to their work by train and, as
luck would have it on this particular morning, it failed to arrive
at its customary time. As a consequence the usual complement
of miners was not present when the explosion occurred and so
the number of casualties was less than what had been initially
reported by the *New York Times*. Of the 89 who had managed to
arrive on time, only five made it out alive.

Such a large disparity in estimating the number of miners lost
was not unheard of, and such was the case when the sole entrance
to the Avondale Mine in Plymouth, Pennsylvania caught fire on
6 September 1869. The initial assumption was that 202 miners
had been trapped without any means of escape. Eight hours were
to go by before the entrance fire could be extinguished and it was
only then that the toxicity of the air could be tested by lowering
a dog in a box. Its survival only provided false hope and in the
end not a single miner was rescued. The only blessing was that

the final count was a much reduced 106. Over 70 of those lost were Welsh and to add to the tragedy was the fact that many of their families were still making their way across the Atlantic and oblivious of what had transpired.

One Briceville family who could consider themselves extremely fortunate on the morning of the Cross Mountain Mine tragedy was that of Henry Davies. He had worked underground ever since his childhood in the Rhondda Valley, and with his 50 years of experience he had become wary of the safety procedures being followed at the Cross Mountain Mine where he had worked for some time. On that very morning he had insisted that his sons accompany him to seek work elsewhere. As to those who didn't share his insight, they have been commemorated in a ballad written by a Thomas Evans:

> The hills around all echoed,
>   As women and children cried;
> This is the song of Cross Mountain mines
>   Where there our brothers died...

CHAPTER 5

Adhering to Welsh Traditions

Social Activities

On referring to Thomas J Davies, a prominent mining superintendent in Oliver Springs, one of his associates expressed concern over his reluctance to arm himself while traversing through the mountainous regions of Tennessee and Kentucky. More than ready to take advantage of one of his stature were those who were referred to as mountain sleders: "The wild occupiers of these mountains have raised fear amongst some of the Pennsylvania bosses, driving them close to losing all perspective" [Mae gwylltiaid y mynyddoedd yma, wedi dychrynu rhai o fosyddion Pennsylvania, a pheri iddynt bron golli arnynt eu hunain]. Jellico itself was as wild as a place could be, with the whisky flowing throughout the day, and someone shot on a weekly basis if not more often. Or so it would appear from what Philip Francis could recall from his years of working at the Dowlais Mine, only a mile away. On approaching his nineties, and after seventy years of labouring underground, he was persuaded by his family to record some of his earlier experiences. Reproduced below is his account of how perilous it could be, even on visiting a barbershop.

> One Saturday evening I went to Jellico for a haircut and shave. The barbershop was near the state line, dividing the town. A young barber there from Cincinnati was doing my work. I was

partly shaved when a fight commenced just outside the door on the pavement. The door was open and the barber could see the fight. His hand trembled so he could not hold the razor. Steady fighting was going on in less than twenty feet in front of us. I could not see them as I reclined in the chair, but I tried to encourage him to finish shaving me.

I told him I did not think that they would bother us. Suddenly he said, his voice trembling, "Oh! He's got him down with his knife in his hand and going to cut his guts out." "Go on and shave me," I said. "I can't," he said, "I'm afraid I'll cut you." Suddenly the fight quieted down and the crowd moved away from in front of the barbershop. I waited a while for the barber to get his composure. He said to me, "I'm going to leave this wild town." As I lay in the chair, he began to lather my cheek again. He had done this several times before, trying to steady his hand. As he was about to commence shaving me, he backed behind the chair. I lifted my head slightly and looked toward the door. There I saw Billie Lyons, one of the worst gunfighters in Kentucky or in Tennessee. He stood in the doorway with two revolvers, one in each hand. He was bare-headed and with blood on his face. He looked desperate. As I was still reclining in the chair, Lyons stepped forward and peered closely into my face and then quickly left. That got the barber to shaking again. Six heavy revolver shots rang out, fired slowly as if at an object, sounding close by. Then it became very quiet again. At last the barber finished shaving me. I was told that he left town the following week. I had been in the chair nearly one hour and a half. All others who were waiting their turn had left.

Given that they were faced with having to contend with such unruly individuals in addition to the recently introduced convicts, one may well ask whether the Welsh, or the *Cymry* (pronounced 'come-ree') as they referred to themselves, might have been better off had they remained clear of Tennessee altogether. Having to live under such dire circumstances could have easily compromised their own social well-being and so the question arises as to how content they could have been, especially as their own cultural background dictated that they themselves should not be the cause of any unseemly behaviour. Yet, despite everything, there is ample evidence to suggest that they did manage to adhere to their traditional way of life, through organizing their own churches, remaining committed to their Sunday schools, and participating in the activities of literary societies and eisteddfod competitions.

The term 'eisteddfod' is derived from the word *eistedd*, to sit, and it implies a sitting or gathering where those in attendance would partake in poetic and musical competitions. These cultural festivals were extremely popular amongst Welsh immigrants during the nineteenth century and a limited amount of information still exits regarding the ones held in Knoxville in 1890 and Chattanooga the following year. Even such time-honoured gatherings as these could also serve as a means of familiarizing themselves with their new environment. As will become apparent later, and instead of harking back to something associated with their background in Wales, many of the main literary competitions at the Chattanooga Eisteddfod, in particular, were orientated towards providing a better understanding of the city's more recent past.

While familiarity with the language would be required to follow a good part of the eisteddfod proceedings, that wouldn't necessarily be a distraction when it came to appreciate the choral competitions. Such competitions had become so well known in certain regions of nineteenth-century America that they were even alluded to in a description of one of the 320 species of birds native to Ohio (*Birds of Ohio*, 1903):

> When the first warm days of March bring up the Bluebirds and Robins, the Juncoes get the spring fever. But they do not rush off to fill premature graves in the still snowy north. The company musters instead in the tree tops on the quiet side of the woods, and indulges in a grand eisteddfod. I am sure the

birds are a little Welch and this term is strictly correct. All
sing at once a sweet little twinkling trill, not very pretentious,
but tender and winsome. Interspersed with this is a variety
of sipping and suchling notes whose use is hard to discern…
During the progress of the concert some dashing young fellow,
unable fully to express his emotion in song, runs amuck…
others catch the infection, and I have seen scores at once in a
mad whirl of this harmless excitement.

The Pennsylvania miners could be as boisterous in support
of their local choirs as they would be at sporting events. A day-
long eisteddfod would often be followed by an evening concert,
and for many of the non-winning participants, it would be a
chance to redeem themselves after their earlier disappointments.
In northern cities such as Milwaukee and Chicago, these
concerts would often attract audiences ranging up to four or five
thousand, totals that exceeded the local Welsh populations. With
Knoxville's upcoming eisteddfod, and from a comment made in
the *Washington Post* (9 October 1890) while referring to another
of the city's events, one gets the impression that others in addition
to the Welsh were likely to attend:

BLUE AND GREY REUNION CLOSED. The reunion
exercises closed here to-night with a magnificent display of
fireworks. Competent judges pronounce it is one of the finest
ever seen in this country. During the week not the slightest
accident occurred to mar the pleasure. Old soldiers of both
armies have had a grand time. It is estimated that thirty to forty
thousand have been in the city. Tomorrow the Welsh citizens
will give an eisteddfod and many of the visitors will remain
for it. Prof. A P Madoc, of Chicago; ex-Postmaster General
James of New York [a cabinet member in President Garfield's
administration] and other notables will attend.

At this particular eisteddfod two contestants were deemed
equally worthy of a prize offered for a poem honouring the

memory of the recently deceased Joseph Richards. Through his success with the iron foundry, he had provided many of them with the opportunity of earning their livelihood in Knoxville. There to lead the eisteddfod proceedings, having travelled all the way from the Mid West to do so, was P E Powell. Better known through his bardic name of Gwilym Eryri, his function was to introduce the contestants and entertain the audience while the adjudicators tallied up their marks. Between his cultural awareness and ready wit, he must have provided an extra dimension to the event.

On 10 October, the eve of his return journey, they honoured him with a special dinner at Knoxville's Shubert Hotel. In attendance were some of Knoxville's leading dignitaries, from David Richards who had succeeded his brother in overseeing the operations of the foundry, to E J Davies, who presided over the East Tennessee Coal Co. Then there was Thomas R Price, who ran the Knoxville Furniture Co., his brother Dr L J Price, and the recently arrived lawyer E D Davies, who had served as secretary to the eisteddfod. Also present were representatives of the Welsh communities in Chattanooga, Louisville and Mahony City. According to one eye witness, "good times were had – a dinner to satisfy the body and a feast to satisfy the mind" [Cawd amser da – ciniaw i'r corff a gwledd i'r meddwl]. A series of toasts were proposed, drawing the wittiest of responses and inspiring Gwilym Eryri to be at his most articulate best. However, even he was surprised when presented with a walking cane with the following engraved on its gold handle: "Presented to Mr P E Powell by the committee of the State Eisteddfod, Knoxville, Tenn., 10 October 1890."

Preparing to compete at the Chattanooga Eisteddfod in the following year was a recently formed choir in Knoxville. Having travelled from Scranton, Pennsylvania to adjudicate in the musical competitions was Daniel Protheroe, a leading choral conductor who had composed the melodies for such well-known hymns as 'Jesus, Lover of my Soul'. As luck would have it, the Knoxville choir could do no better than come second to a choir from Soddy under the leadership of a Joseph Lloyd. In 1893, their Knoxville Male Chorus ventured as far north as Chicago to compete in an eisteddfod that had been arranged as part of the festivities during the city's World Fair.

As to the Cymdeithas Gymrodorol Knoxville (the Welsh Society of Knoxville), some preliminary discussions regarding its formation had taken place at the time of the 1890 eisteddfod. However, it would not be formally organized until November of the following year. On 26 March 1892, its members were given the opportunity of hearing David Richards, Joseph Richards's brother, discuss the extent of the Welsh participation in the Civil War. Also on hand to help enlighten them on the same evening was David Groves, and given his early perseverance with the mill in Lauden, who better to reminisce about 'The Welsh in Tennessee before and during the Civil War'. When it came to election time, David Richards would take up the cause of the Republican Party, addressing his listeners in English or Welsh, as the occasion demanded. Many a time he had stood on the steps of Knoxville's courthouse, espousing the merits of the Republican Party, on occasion with his teenage son as his sole listener. At the urging of others, he reluctantly agreed to serve one term in the Tennessee State Legislature.

Another much admired member of their Knoxville community was a sister of Joseph Parry, Wales's foremost music composer. He had once worked in the rolling mills of Danville, Pennsylvania alongside some of those who would later relocate to Knoxville. His rise to prominence as a musician followed his return to his native Wales. Given that his sister was referred to as "a singer of great renown", one can safely assume that she would have participated in the entertainment during the society's gatherings. Then to be

called upon for their entertainment in the Jellico area were the
choir and brass band that had been organized within months of
their arrival in Mountain Ash: "The old mountains of Kentucky
resonate to the tunes sung by the Welsh sons and daughters, and
there to saturate the breezes are the varying accented sounds of
their band" [Dadseinia hen fynyddau Kentucky y tonau a genir
gan y meibion a'r merched Cymreig, a llenwir col yr awelon gan
acenion amryfal y seindorf].

As was often the case in nineteenth-century Wales, perusal of
religious understanding would continue to dominate the lives of
many. Between their tendency to gauge their own lives in Biblical
terms and, the long-held belief that they as a nation had helped
protect Christianity through its darker days, one can appreciate
the deep-felt sentiments expressed by one individual who had
made it to Knoxville as early as 1867:

> Yr ydym, er pan ddaethom yma, wedi mwynhau cysuron
> ysbrydol a thymhorol yn helaeth, ac y mae daioni a thiriondeb
> y Nef tuag atom yn fawr, fel y gellir ein cyffelybu ar rai
> ystyriaethau i hiliogaeth Heber, y genedl honno a neillduwyd
> i gadw coffadwriaeth o enw Ior ar y ddaear. Hwy oeddynt
> bobl briodol Jehofa cyn dyfodiad y Messiah. Hiliogaeth Gomer
> ydynt mewn modd neillduol yn gyffelyb, oherwydd nid oes
> un genedl oddi ar oes yr Apostolion wedi cadw'r Efengyl mor
> ddilwgr a'r genedl Gymreig. Er mai nifer fechan sydd yma yn
> bresenol, mae yma rai eto heb gael adnabyddiaeth o'r gwir a'r
> bywiol Dduw; Bydded i Dduw chwythu'r awelon yn dyner
> drosom, a disgyned y gwlith yn esmwyth arnom; a'r Duw
> hwnnw fu yn gwylied plant Israel yn Gosen, a ofalo am Gymry
> Knoxville.

> [*We have, since our arrival here, enjoyed spiritual and seasonal
> comforts, and the goodness and gentleness of Heaven towards us
> has been great, so that we can be compared in some respects to the
> descendants of Heber, that nation who was set apart to keep alive on
> earth the name of the Lord. They were the proper Jehovah people before*

the coming of the Messiah. The descendants of Gomer [grandson of Noah and from whom the Welsh were once believed to have descended] are in a unique way similar, as there is not a single nation since the Apostles who have kept the Gospel as uncorrupted as the Welsh nation. Though we are only few here at present, there are some who are yet to gain knowledge of the true and living God... May God direct a gentle breeze over us, and let the dew bring comfort; and that God who watched over the children of Israel in Goshen, may he also care for the Knoxville Welsh.]

Welsh-language Churches

Before attempting to summarize what is known of their churches in Tennessee and the bordering part of Kentucky, it is worth noting that the vast majority of the 600 or so Welsh-language churches that once flourished in the United States were primarily based in the more northern part of the country. This becomes apparent on glancing over a list of such churches compiled by Edward Hartmann and included at the end of his 1967 authoritative book, *Americans from Wales*. Not a single one appears under Kentucky and only two under Tennessee. The presence of additional churches in both states is suggested by a few passing remarks regarding their various religious activities. The following provides what limited evidence there is regarding their formation, as well as expanding on what is more generally known about the two churches referred to by Hartmann in his book.

Unlike many other denominations, the Congregational Church encourages individual churches to persue a course of action without first seeking the approval of some central authority. Such a loose affiliation amongst its churches makes it far easier for prospective members to start a church of their own and the very first of such churches in Tennessee was the one organized in Knoxville in February 1870. Prior to that time they had held their meetings through the generosity of one of the city's existing churches (second Presbytarian). The following account from *Y Cenhadwr Americanaidd* [The American Missionary] indicates that a good many of the 104 who were regarded as being the earliest arrivals were present at a special Christmas gathering in 1867:

Treuliasom y Nadolig yn ddifyrus dros ben. Cawsom gwrdd yma am 2 o'r gloch prydhawn, er rhoddi mantais i'r plant i adrodd eu darnau pwrpasol, ac i ganu. Yr oedd lleisiau soniarus a naturiol y rhai bach yn swnio yn ein clustiau yn fwynaidd, ac yn effeithio ar bob calon, nes oedd dagrau o orfoledd yn dylifo dros ruddiau llawer. Cawsom hefyd yr anrhydedd o gael David Richards, Ysw., Columbia, Pa., yn ein plith yn y cyfarfod. Traddododd araeth ddyddorol a phwrpasol yn ei ddull tanllyd a hyawdl. Mae Mr Richards yn Gymro trwyadl. Cafwyd amryw benillion gan yr enwog fardd Thomas Davies ar ei ymadewiad o Columbia, Pa. Cafwyd amryw donau gan y cor dan arweiniad William Lewis. Hefwyd cafwyd araeth ardderchog gan Mr Joseph Richards, "Gofal Duw am Gymry Knoxville", yn ei ddull mwynaidd a syml. Canodd Wm J Richards ddernyn – mae amryw yn y gogledd, tua Pennsylvania, yn gwybod pa fath ganwr yw. Canodd John Richards, ar y geiriau, "Wele cawsom y Messiah," &c., yn yr hen ddull, yn effeithiol iawn…

[*We spent Christmas in a very joyful way. A service was held at 2 o'clock in the afternoon so that the children could recite their special pieces, and to sing. The sonorus and natural voices of the little ones was sweetness to our ears, affecting every heart, drawing tears of rejoicement over many a cheek. We were also honoured by the presence in our midst of David Richards, Esq., Columbia, Pa. He provided us with an interesting and purposeful talk in his fiery and eloquent way. Mr Richards is a thorough Welshman. Several stanzas were provided by the noted poet Thomas Davies on his departure from Columbia, Pa. Several songs were provided by the choir under the leadership of William Lewis. Joseph Richards, in his gentle way, spoke magnificently of "God's care of Knoxville's Welsh". Wm J Richards sang a piece – many in the north, around Pennsylvania, know the sort of singer he is. John Richards was very effective in singing in the old fashioned way, "Wele cawsom y Messiah," &c…*]

Their services were held initially not in the main church building but in an adjacent room and they would meet just prior to the main service. On becoming enthralled with their singing, others would attend and this occurred despite their lack of understanding the language. As a consequence, the Welsh services had to be moved into the main church itself and, apart from the singing, the enlarged congregation may have been exposed to a more dynamic form of preaching which differed significantly from the English tradition of tediously reading from pre-written sermon notes. A well-known account relates how a Welsh preacher had been invited to give the opening sermon at a joint gathering of the Congregational Churches of England and Wales. Once in London, and fearing that he had to adhere to English practices, he inquired as to whether he was expected to arm himself with notes. On being told that that would not be necessary as long as he retained his "Welsh fire", he responded by stating that perhaps he should take notes to the pulpit but use them as "kindling paper". So for anybody accustomed to Welsh preaching, a typical English sermon would be dullness to the extreme.

Many of the Welsh ministers of the period could capture the attention of even the most inattentive worshiper and, on referring to one of his former fellow ministers in Pennsylvania, their second pastor in Knoxville mentioned how "on the most dry of times he can draw rain from the clouds of heaven" [Ar yr amser sychaf gall dyny glaw o gymylau y nef]. Most bewildering of all for any outsider who sat through one of their sermons in Knoxville would have been the more frenzied delivery on coming to the climactic part of the sermon. A description of this peculiarity is provided in an article published in *Wallace's Monthly* in 1876. The author, Erasmus Jones, was himself a preacher and had served as chaplain to an African-American regiment during the Civil War:

The effect often produced by a popular Welsh preacher is wonderful. There is one peculiarity connected with their preaching which differs entirely from anything that I ever observed in English pulpits; it is usually marked by a great variety of intonations. I do not know the origin of this chanting style of preaching... it differs entirely from that monotonous tone that is often heard in English churches, or the chromatic chanting of the mass before papal altars. It is a melody of the purest nature... the best description I can give of this peculiarity is this: It is the application of sentences in a chanting style to portions of the minor scale. The minister is never at a loss how to apply the words to the melody; they appear to run together as by mutual attraction. The sentence is started, for instance, on E minor. The minister has his own peculiar melody. It ranges here and there from the first to the fifth, often reaching the octave, and then descending and ending in sweet cadence on the key note.

Their lifelong familiarity with such preaching would only add to their desire for forming their own separate church. While their initial membership was only 62, they usually managed to attract a congregation that ranged from 80 to approaching a 100. It was around this time that a certain Rev. Thomas Thomas happened to be visiting the city, his sole reason for doing so being that he was on his way to visit a brother in Shelby, Alabama whom he had not seen for 37 years. Born in Pen-y-bont ar Ogwr in 1808, he had continued to live in Wales until undertaking this trip as a 62 year-old in 1870. Prior to becoming a minister he had worked as a puddler, first in Aberdare and then in Pencae (Ebbw Vale) and, given that two of the elders of the newly-formed church were also from Ebbw Vale, he had all the right credentials for being invited to become their very first minister.

The church itself was built on land acquired for a minimal amount from the Knoxville Iron & Coal Co. Twenty years on, when the building underwent renovation, E J Davies of the East

Tennessee Coal Co. was generous enough to donate a dollar for every dollar collected. By the second Sunday of 1893 it was ready for its rededication: "According to its size it is today one of the most beautiful churches in the city of Knoxville" [Yn ôl ei faint y mae heddiw yn un o'r capeli harddaf yn nhref hardd Knoxville]. Sadly, it would not survive that much longer and, by the time a memorial service was held in it for David Richards who died at the age of 81 in 1906, it was no longer a Welsh Congregational Church but one that belonged to the United Bretheren.

The Knoxville church was one of the two recognized by Professor Edward Hartmann as being in Tennessee, and his awareness of its presence is hardly surprising in view of his often expressed admiration for their second minister, the Rev. D R Thomas. Generally referred to by his assumed literary name of Iorthyn Gwynedd, he is remembered not only for his ministry but for his monumental effort in gathering information on the extent and nature of Welsh American settlements. Still as significant as ever is his *Hanes Cymry America* [History of the Welsh in America] which was published in 1872, the year of his arrival in Knoxville. Soon afterwards he expressed his satisfaction at having moved to the city:

> Prynasom dy newydd hardd a chyfleus yno, a dodrefnasom
> ef yn y modd goreu. Yr oedd fy anwyl briod a'm plant yn
> hoffi dinas Knoxville, a'r eglwys Gymreig, a'u cartref newydd
> yn fawr iawn, ac yr oedd pawb o'n cyfeillion yn hoff iawn
> ohonynt hwythau. Ni welais eglwysi mor unol, mor ffyddlon,
> ac mor wresog… bu yr Anrh. David Richards, a'i frodyr Joseph
> Richards ysw., a William J. Richards ysw., (sef perchnogion y
> Rolling Mill a'r gweithiau glo) yn gyfeillion mynwesol i mi a'm
> teulu… Sabbath Ebrill 13, 1873 agorwyd ein capel newydd yn
> Knoxville.
>
> [*We bought a beautiful and conveniently located home there [on Clark
> St, Mechanicsville], and furnished it in the best way. My dear wife*

and children liked Knoxville, the Welsh Church, and their new home very much, and all of our friends were very fond of them. I never saw churches so united, faithful, and with such warmth… the Hon. David Richards, his brothers Joseph Richards Esq., and William J Richards Esq., (owners of the Rolling Mill and coal works) were bosom friends to me and my family… Sabboth 13 April 1873 saw the opening of our new church building in Knoxville.]

His use of 'churches' rather than 'a church' is presumably a referral to the associated church in Coal Creek. As several of the church members, including Joseph Richards himself, had left Knoxville for Chattanooga just prior to his arrival, he was faced with a membership that had dwindled down to as low as 45 to 50. Yet, within a few months, Iorthyn Gwynedd had succeeded in getting another 28 or so to join and, according to an article published in December 1872 by the *Knoxville Daily Chronicle*, church-related functions were being held on practically every night of the week. On Tuesday nights one could attend the young men's meeting, Wednesday nights the children's meeting (with David Richards assisting the minister), Thursday nights a prayer meeting and Friday nights an evening of song.

Intent on having his book *Hanes Cymry America* [History of the Welsh in America] published in Wales as well, Iorthyn Gwynedd set out on a return visit in the following spring. Accompanied by a William G Lewis, their train journey would take them through Bristol, Tennessee and Lynchburg, Virginia before proceeding through Washington and on to Philadelphia. There Iorthyn Gwynedd interrupted his journey so that he could preach to his former congregation in Mahanoy City. He finally sailed from New York on 20 April and, as there were many others of Welsh descent on the same voyage, he was called upon to preach on several occasions. He arrived in Liverpool on 8 May and despite being warmly welcomed wherever he went, he never succeeded in getting his book republished. Adding to his anxiety was his wife's failure to respond to several of his letters. It was not until his return journey, and when he was met in New York and given a letter from the eldest of his three children, that he became aware of how she had passed away in the meantime:

> Knoxville, Tenn., 30 July 1873. Dear Papa, We received your kind and loving letters. But oh! How it makes my heart ache to think you are writing to one whom you suppose alive, but is dead! One whom we all loved...

As was the case with Iorthyn Gwynedd, many of those who had relocated to the Knoxville area had once resided in Mahanoy City, Pennsylvania. About 1,000 of its inhabitants were thought to be Welsh and they constituted the majority of those who eventually settled in Dowlais, Kentucky. So wherever Iorthyn Gwynedd preached in the Knoxville area, he would invariably meet somebody or other who had come to know him during his former ministry. Amongst those from Mahanoy City to take up residence in Knoxville itself was the school teacher Elizabeth Jeffries who would later marry E J Davies of the East Tennessee Coal Co. During the strike of 1875, when many were forced to seek employment elsewhere, Iorthyn Gwynedd departed for Columbus, Ohio and he remained there until 1877. On his return, he became their pastor once more and he continued in that capacity until his retirement in 1881. On his death in 1888, he was buried alongside his wife at Knoxville's Old Gray Cemetry and whatever was engraved in smaller lettering towards the bottom of their headstone has long since eroded.

To be found grouped together some 30 yards away from his resting place are the headstones of many of the city's earlier Welsh. The Welsh inscription seen on a number of them is about the only reminder of how their language had once flourished in Knoxville's Mechanicsville section. Just about readable on the headstone of a John G Evans from Meirionethshire, who died in 1884, are the words 'Gwyn eu byd y meirw y rhai sydd yn marw yn yr Arglwydd' (Revelation 14:13: 'Blessed are the dead who die in the Lord'). Also in the same vicinity are the graves of two of the Richards' brothers, David and William, with the latter having once served as choral director to several of the city's leading churches. The failure to locate the grave of the third brother Joseph only became apparent later and on realizing that he had spent the latter part of his life in Oliver Springs.

The place name of Dowlais in Wales is all too apparent at the New Gray Cemetery where yet more are buried. Quoted on the headstone of a Sarah Phillip Humphries is the Biblical verse 'Canys byw i mi yw Crist a marw sydd elw' (Philippians 1:21: 'For me to live is Christ, and to die is gain'). Also buried in the same vicinity are William Eynon from Merthyr and his wife Jane from Llanelli, an Evan Jones from Merthyr and his wife Letita from Aberdare. Then there are the Leyshons, with Thomas born in Mahonoy, Pa., Margaret Humphries Leyshon in Dowlais, and a sister of the latter whose name is given as Gwenllian Simpon. As to the Philip Francis, whose expertise was called upon after the 1902 mine explosion, he was laid to rest in a mausoleum of his own construction in the Lynhurst Cemetery. Until recently, his former home had remained in the possession of the family and today it still gives the appearance of having once been one of the more elegant homes in all of Knoxville.

The second of their Tennessee churches was the one referred to as being organized in Coal Creek in 1870, around the same time as the one in Knoxville itself. Their initial services were held in a hall-like building that belonged to the mine, and a year or more went by before they managed to erect the church. As in Knoxville, the Rev. Thomas Thomas became their first minister and, after another period under the guidance of Iorthyn Gwynedd, they ordained one of their own members, a Rev. G W Smith who was from Mynydd Islwyn in Monmouthshire.

Prior to becoming a minister, he had been a miner and in 1877 he left the Coal Creek area to become the pastor of another Welsh church in Soddy. Affiliated with the Coal Creek Church was a Literary and Temperance Society and briefly mentioned in the February 1875 issue of *Y Cenhadwr Americanaidd* is how the Welsh of Tennessee had held meetings:

> … er cefnogi llenyddiaeth a cherddoriaeth Gymreig, ac egwyddori plant yr ysgolion Sabbothol yn yr Ysgrythurau, gan Gymry Tennessee, yn Knoxville Rhag. 25, 1874 ac yn Coal Creek, Anderson Co., Tennessee, Ion. 1, 1875.

> [… *so as to be supportive of Welsh literature and music, and to instruct the children of the Sabbath schools in the Scriptures, in Knoxville on Dec. 25, 1874, and in Coal Creek, Anderson Co., Tennessee on January 1, 1875.*]

As content as they had been until around this time in Coal Creek, things took a dramatic turn for the worse soon afterwards. Over the coming months they had to endure not only the hardships associated with a strike, but also the presence of the convicts brought to their midst. Between the departure of many from the area and the degrading influence of the convicts, the church could no longer sustain itself. Sometime around 1890 it was reopened for conducting a Sunday school, but it never regained its former influence on the community. Whatever its eventual fate, another church still survives four miles away in Briceville. Locally, it is regarded as having been built by Welsh miners in 1888. A nearby historic marker states:

> Built in 1888 by immigrant Welsh coalminers, Briceville Church and Cemetery were added to the National Register of Historic Places in August 2003. It is one of the oldest structures remaing in Anderson County.

On continuing northward from Coal Creek, and crossing the state line into Kentucky, their religious aspirations become apparent once more, from Dowlais to Proctor and Mountain Ash – all in the vicinity of Jellico – and to as far afield as Baxtertown 40 miles away. Confirming the existence of a church in Proctor is an account of how the choir and brass band from Mountain Ash had helped defray its construction cost through holding a concert there in 1892. And when Mountain Ash itself was visited by David Richards, one hears of how he "had led us in the Sunday School proceedings and provided us with an excellent address" [athrawodd yn yr Ysgol Sul i ni, a chawsom anerchiad campus ganddo]. Here it is worth noting that as the Welsh language was prohibited in the state schools of Wales itself, the so-called 'Sunday schools' had taken on a special significance – they had become the means of acquiring literacy in one's own language.

On the first Sunday of 1893, which so happened to be New Year's Day as well, the Mountain Ash Choir would once again respond to the need of a church. They were called upon to take part in the consecration of a church 40 miles away in Baxtertown. Travelling by train, they were said to have entertained themselves along the way by singing traditional Welsh hymns. On this historic occasion, sermons were given in both English and Welsh and amongst those who valued their singing were a number "who had been deprived from hearing a Welsh song for ten to fifteen years" [nid oedd rhai ohonynt wedi clywed na chan Gymraeg o'r blaen ers o 10 i 15 mlynedd].

Even though Dowlais was the first of the various communities in the Jellico area, there is no clear indication as to whether a church was ever built there. Yet Philip Francis mentions how Welsh-language services were being held within a year or so of his arrival. He also noted how sweet the children sang and how they were often called upon to sing in churches not affiliated with the Welsh. The most compelling reason for believing that a church did indeed exist in Dowlais is a passing reference to a one-legged miner named Jonathan Jenkins, who rang a church

bell on Sundays (he later moved to Mountain Ash on becoming
a superintendent). Without the unifying influence of a church,
it is also unlikely that they would have managed to organize an
eisteddfod to celebrate St David's Day in 1890. Victorious in a
competition that asked for six stanzas on St David was a Howell
Davies from Coal Creek (he later relocated to the Jellico area).
In the first of his six verses, he expressed the sentiment of how St
David (Dewi, the son of Sandde) had flourished after the Romans
(Rhufeinwyr) withdrew from Britain (Prydain), and devoted his
life to spreading the gospel amongst his beloved Welsh:

> Duwiol-ddyn yn caru ei gyd-ddyn a'i wlad
> Yn annwyl oedd Dewi ap Sandde;
> Blodeuodd ar ôl i'r Rhufeinwr a'i gad
> Ddychwelid o Brydain i'w gartre',
> Pregethai'r efengyl yn ffyddlon trwy'i oes,
> A gwelodd yr had da yn gwreiddio,
> A thyfu yn ffrwythlon yn hinsawdd y groes,
> Lle'r hoffai ei enaid breswylio.

The second of the two churches in Tennessee that was referred
to by Edward Hartmann was the one that came into being in
Soddy in 1873. By the end of that year, and after initially holding
their services in a hall that belonged to the mining company,
they erected a building which also functioned as a school. Here
again, and as had been the case in Knoxville and Coal Creek, it
was the Rev. Thomas Thomas who saw the church through its
initial period. He probably joined them shortly after the church
was first organized and, on his retirement in 1877, he continued
to live in Soddy. He was succeeded by the previously mentioned
Rev. George W Smith but, after a couple of years, he left to take
charge of another church in Oliver Springs. This brings up the
possibility that a Welsh church might have existed there as well.
However, George W Smith eventually returned to his former
church in Soddy and he continued to live there up to the time

of his death in the early 1890s. The two mentioned ministers were by no means the only ones to dedicate themselves to the Welsh communities in Tennessee, but from their ministries alone it becomes apparent that such churches were very much attuned to each others' needs.

By the early 1880s, their church in Soddy was no longer considered large enough to meet their needs, and it was eventually replaced by a larger 60 by 40-foot building. Towards the end of 1882 concern was expressed over whether it could be completed in time for an eisteddfod that had been scheduled for the Christmas period. Being that it was used for a Sunday school's quarterly meeting on the first Sunday of the following year, it appears that they did indeed manage to meet the eisteddfod deadline after all.

As to the quarterly meeting itself, one of the more pleasing aspects would have been to hear the smaller children recite as many as four chapters out of *Rhodd Mam* [Mother's Gift]. This popular Sunday school text for younger children had been republished in the United States in 1858 and possibly afterwards as well. Visiting Soddy just prior to the completion of the new church was the Rev. Lot Lake of Scranton, Pennsylvania and the fact that some miners had come there directly from Wales caught his attention. Their presence would have undoubtedly helped re-enforce the nature of the community:

> Pobl o Aberdar a Chwm Rhondda sydd yno gan mwyaf, ac nid ydynt wedi eu hanner, na'u chwarter Americaneiddio, ond maent bron yn hollol yn eu cyflwr Cymruyddol. Nid ydynt wedi dechrau siarad yn drwyadl, na therfynu eu hymadroddion rhyw hanner dwsin o raddau yn uwch na'r fan y maent yn eu dechrau; ond y mae eu hacen a'u tonyddiaeth yn hollol Gymruyddol, neu yn fwy cywir, Aberdaraidd. Teimlais fy hun am Sabboth, beth bynnag, fel pe yn byw yng Nghwm Rhondda neu Blaenllechau.

[*To a large extent the people are from Aberdare and the Rhondda
Valley, and they haven't by half, or by quarter become Americanized,
remaining almost completely in their Welsh ways. They haven't started
to speak thoroughly or terminate their saying without being some half a
dozen grades above where they started; but their accent and intonation
remains completely Welsh, or more correctly, Aberdare-like. For a
Sunday at least I felt as if I was living in the Rhondda Valley or
Blaenllechau.*]

Also referred to by the Rev. Lot Lake was another nearby mine
at a place known as Rock Creek. It was under the ownership of
the Soddy Mine and responsible for its day to day operations
was a W Lloyd who had formerly lived in Mahanoy City,
Pennsylvania. As with Soddy itself, the majority of the miners
were Welsh and this enabled them to conduct a Sunday school
in their own language. However, the occasional church services
held there were primarily in English.

Given the significant Welsh presence in Chattanooga, one
may well ask whether they too had managed to start a church
of their own. Residing there in addition to those associated
with the iron industry was a limited number who had risen to
prominence by becoming successful merchants. Considered to be
amongst the city's wealthiest was the highly respected D D Jones,
who owned the well-known bookstore Cady & Co. Originally
from Ruthin, he had once worked at the slate quarries of Middle
Granville in New York State and then moved to Chattanooga
after serving with the Union Army during the Civil War. Most of
his accumulated wealth had come not through his bookstore but
from his expertise in handling slate and the roofing of buildings.
Another of the more prominent store owners was John Lindsay,
and while many considered him to be Scots-Irish, his mother
was Welsh and he could converse in the language as readily as
any of them. But, unlike Knoxville, where the majority were
grouped together in the Mechanicsville section, here they were

much more widely dispersed and favoured attending various neighbourhood churches. It would appear that the nearest they ever got to establishing their own church was the occasional sermon preached in Welsh whenever the Rev. Thomas Thomas happened to be on a visit from Soddy.

With Wales having been endowed with more than its share of religous revivals, the importance of its religious leaders cannot be over emphasized. As in Wales, one could expect that the likes of the Rev. Thomas Thomas, Rev. D R Thomas, Rev. George W Smith and Rev. Lot Lake (who later became their minister in Knoxville) would have exerted considerable influence over Tennessee's Welsh. For many of the age, the fulfillment of their spiritual needs would have matched, if not surpassed, their desire to take care of their physical well-being. Even the word 'moddion' for 'medicine' is often applied to what one acquires through attending church rather than what is prescribed by medical practitioners.

Nevertheless, having access to a Welsh-speaking doctor when confronted with a physical ailment would also be reassuring to many. One who adequately fulfilled such a role was a Dr George William Roberts who had received his medical training in Cincinnati. Born in Ironton, Ohio in 1864, he arrived in Tennessee in 1885 and joined up with Dr L J Price, another doctor of Welsh decent, who was then practicing in Coal Creek. That association led to him being offered a similar position with the East Tennessee Coal Co. in the Jellico area but ultimately he would work for the mining company in Soddy. If nothing else, his career serves to illustrate that on occasion the mine operators did indeed take an interest in the welfare of their workers. Once in Soddy he was invited to become the conductor of their brass band and, in 1887, he married a daughter of W J Williams, one of the mine's principal owners.

The Chattanooga Celebration of 1891

From the following comments this Chattanooga gathering appears to have been the most ambitious and successful of all their festivities in Tennessee:

> Gweler canoedd o Gymry glanedig yn rhodio ystrydoedd Chattanooga, gan lygadu ar ryfeddodau a swynion y dref chwaethus a chyflym-gynyddol hon. Gwelir yma Gymry o ryw ddeg o Daleithiau – Illinois, Pennsylvania, Ohio, Kentucky, West Virginia, Virginia, Carolina, Georgia, Alabama, ac wrth reswm, o Tennessee, talaith enedigol *Eisteddfod Dixie*.

> [*See the hundreds of holy Welshfolk roaming the streets of Chattanooga, taking in the sights and the charms of this elegant and ever-growing city. To be seen here are the Welsh from about ten different states – Illinois, Pennsylvania, Ohio, Kentucky, West Virginia, Virginia, Carolina, Georgia, Alabama, and of course, Tennessee, the birth place of the* Dixie Eisteddfod.]

Their activities were centered around an eisteddfod scheduled for 30 October 1891 and, amongst those making their presence felt, was a contingent from the mountains (mynyddoedd) of Kentucky, anxiously anticipating the event and capable of exhibiting "Pure Welsh (Pur Gymraeg) on every tongue (ar pob tafod)":

> O Kentucky a'i mynyddoedd,
> Gyda chynwrf a llawenfloedd,
> Daw pob Cymro i'r eisteddfod,
> Pur Gymraeg fydd ar pob tafod.

Not everybody who exhibited such fluency in the language were native to Wales and in the case of the E D Davies who had acted as secretary for the earlier eisteddfod in Knoxville, his place of birth was Gallia County, Ohio. From there he had gone to Cincinnati to be educated in the law. For those born in Tennessee, one need not look further than the children of W J

Williams in Soddy – all of the six had been raised through the medium of Welsh.

Amongst those from Chattanooga who were expected to make their presence felt, and 'bubbling with elequence' [byrlymu huawdledd] at that, was the Honorable Henry Clay Evans. Brought up in Wisconsin, he had served as a corporal with the 41st Regiment, Wisconsin Volunteer Infantry, during the Civil War and then settled in Chattanooga in 1870. From 1874 to 1884 he had worked for the Roane Iron Company, serving as secretary, treasurer, and finally vice-president and general manager. Elected as Chattanooga's mayor in 1881, he is credited with organizing the city's public school system. By 1887 he was the principal stockholder and manager of the Chattanooga Car and Foundry Company who specialized in building freight cars. He also served one term in Congress.

Three miles south of the city, and to capture the imagination of every visitor, was the majestic Lookout Mountain. Making its peak readily accessible was an inclined railway whose carriages had been built by Henry Clay Evans's company. As spectacular a view as it afforded of the surrounding countryside, this was only one aspect of what the mountain had to offer. On being posted there as a scout during the Civil War, one Welshman had become enthralled by it all:

> Safai uwchlaw yr holl fynyddoedd cylchol, fel y gellid ar ddiwrnod clir weled drostynt i bellter o gan' milltir, a chanfod manau amlwg mewn saith o wahanol daleithiau. Ymddangosai yr holl amgylchoedd yn fawreddus o donog a garw… Ond ni byddai golygfeydd y diwrnod clir i'w cymharu a golygfeydd y cymylau. Byddai niwl a chymylau tewion yn gorchuddio y wlad bron bob bore, ac yn aml ar amserau eraill, ond ymestynai pen y mynydd uwchlaw iddynt oll, fel na byddai ond tu uchaf y cymylau yn ymddangos i ni mewn awyr glir, a'r haul gyda thanbeidrwydd gogoneddus yn pelydru arnynt…

[*It stands above all of the surrounding mountains, so that on a clear day one can see over them to a distance of a hundred miles, and discover noteworthy places in seven different states. The entire surroundings give the impression of a rough and undulating grandeur... But the sights on a clear day didn't begin to compare with the view of the clouds. Covering the countryside nearly every morning, and often at other times, were dense clouds and fog, but the mountain's peak managed to reach above them all, so that only the topside of the clouds would appear to us in a clear sky, and with the sun's splendid fire casting its rays on it all.*]

Such were the circumstances in 1863 when the so-called Battle above the Clouds had been fought, with the Confederates occupying Lookout Mountain and the Unionists a lesser peak but which also managed to pierce through the clouds. For hours cannon balls flowed back and forth through the clear sky above, with the Confederates feeling invincible in view of their higher elevation. But, unknown to them, and making their way up through the cloud cover were Union soldiers, who managed to catch them unaware. This led to many of the Confederates being driven over the cliffs to their eventual death – something that is alluded to by Gwerfil James in one of the eisteddfod's competitions which called for four *englyn*-type stanzas to Lookout Mountain:

> Mantell i'r Lookout Mountain – yw gwyrddion,
> Geindeg erddi bychain,
> Gwyllt flodau, llysiau'n mhob llain –
> Mieri a llus mirain.
>
> Dyrcha'i ben i'r wybrenau – ar ei war
> Myn eryrod chwarau;
> A llu'n eu hoen, tra'n llawenhau
> A'i dringant, dremiant o'i drumiau.
>
> Pam o'em heb undeb, er bendith – y wlad,
> Hwn fu'n lys meib rhagrith,
> Er cryfhau y pleidiau'n ein plith,
> Er mallter, rhyfel, a melldith.

Ein milwyr uwch ei gymylau – faeddynt
    Garn fyddin y Dehau
    Nes heb god y giwod gau
    Llithrent i'w tranc o'i lethrau!

The first stanza sets the scene, with the variety of gardens and the proliferation of wild flowers and berries, all unifying to provide the mountain with a colourful mantle. The second stanza directs one's attention to the soaring eagles above, whose persistency laid claim to the mountain as a place for their rejoicement alone. All such tranquility is cast aside by the opening line of the third stanza – 'when we were without a Union for the good of the land'. What follows goes on to express how the mountain had suddenly been turned into a court that stood in judgement over 'the sons of hypocrisy'. In the final stanza one hears of the Confederates' ultimate demise, with many meeting their death through being driven over the precipices. Not only does the poet capture in relatively few words what Lookout Mountain had come to represent, but he managed to do so while adhering to a complex rhythmic pattern known as 'cynghanedd': embedded in every line is either an alliterative pattern or an internal rhyming scheme.

The eisteddfod's main choral competition was open to choirs whose number fell within the range of 50 to 75. As much as $100 was being offered in prize money for the best rendition of the 'Hallelujah Chorus'. For those who had travelled to Chattanooga from smaller communities, there was always the possibility of participating in some of the less prestigious competitions. The set-piece for choirs whose number fell between 35 and 50 was 'Y Blodeuyn Olaf' [The Last Flower], with the corresponding prize money reduced to $50. For choirs of no more than 30 voices, as much as $40 was being offered for singing 'Nant y Mynydd' [The Mountain Creek]. The following verse reveals how three leading choirs had expressed a desire to participate in the main choral competition. Not only that, but the last couplet goes on to boast that there wasn't a choir throughout the entire northern states (gogledd-dir) that could 'hold a candle' (canwyll) to what they had to offer in the South!

> Dod i ganu'r 'Haleliwia',
> A wnai tri o'r gorau gora',
> Nid oes gorau trwy'r gogledd-dir,
> Ddeil y ganwyll i'r Deheudir.

The fact that the Welsh excelled when it came to choral singing became apparent to the Jubilee Singers when they undertook a concert tour of Europe in 1873. This group consisted of students from the newly-formed African-American Fisk University in Nashville and, at one stage, their performances were close to being the sole contributor to the school's revenue. After a few indifferent appearances, their initial success came when they resorted to singing in a style that reflected their own culture and that in front of a gathering of clergymen at Oberlin College in Ohio. On 7 August 1873, and at the time of their fund-raising European tour, the following reference to the singing abilities of the Welsh appeared in the African-American publication, *The Christian Record* :

> What the relation of the Negro to the Welsh is, we are not exactly informed. That there is some relation, to our mind, is clear. The reason wherefore is that both sing. Didn't the man whose great-grandfather sold Gen. Washington a horse claim a relationship to him? Why then can't we claim a relationship to the Welsh, or they to us. Griffith Jones, or as he is better known, Caradoc, of Aberdare, south Wales, with his Welsh choir, recently carried off from the Crystal Palace the $5,000 Gold Cup; and that too, despite the efforts of three million London.
>
> We suggest. Let these Welsh singers unite with our Jubilee songster now in England and give a concert in London. Verily the days of Julien and of Jenny Lind would be eclipsed.

The name of Griffith Rhys Jones, who defied the odds by taking a mass choir of 460 miners and iron workers to compete against the better endowed choirs of England, is still revered locally in the Aberdare area. His former home is still referred to as Llety Caradog (dwelling of Caradog) and not often does a local community unite to erect a statue to one who earned his livelihood as a humble blacksmith. The Crystal Palace associated with the competition had initially been built to house the Great Exhibition of 1851, the very first World Fair. His victory in 1872 was repeated in the following year and, shortly before that, complimentary remarks appeared in *The Christian Record*.

Not long after the termination of the Second World War, the small market town of Llangollen in north Wales became host to a variation on the traditional eisteddfod. Focusing on dance and song, various ethnic groups, many of whom had been decimated by the war, were invited to come and meet in friendly competiton. It continues to be held on an annual basis and has grown into the highly acclaimed Llangollen International Folk Eisteddfod with worldwide participation. Yet they were not the first to welcome an outside ethnic group to participate at an eisteddfod, and here pride of place must go to Chattanooga. Incorporated into their 1891 eisteddfod was a competition for the best performance of what was described as the Polish National Dance.

Through making Lookout Mountain the subject of the previously referred competition, the eisteddfod became a means of enhancing their understanding of Tennessee's immediate past. This would not be the only competition to serve such a purpose and there to adjudicate over the literary competitions in general was the Rev. Gwrhyd Lewis from Wilkes-Barre, Pennsylvania. His most daunting task would be to decide on who should be awarded the much coveted handcrafted armchair with all its symbolic carvings, and that was being offered for a longer poem commemorating the feats of the Civil War general, George Thomas.

Earlier in the war, and alongside a church called Siloh in the western part of the state, each side had suffered the loss of over 10,000 of their troops. Then, a year and a half later, and in the final months of 1863, General George Thomas achieved national acclaim after a series of battles fought in the vicinity of Chattanooga itself. Twelve miles south, in a narrow ravine called Chickamauga, it was he alone of the Union generals who had managed to hold his ground, a feat that led to him being referred to as the Rock of Chickamauga. Then, in the aftermath of the battle fought on Lookout Mountain itself, and despite the presence of both Hooker and Grant, it was his battle weary troops who ultimately drove the Confederates from their encampment on the nearby Missionary Ridge. In the following year he again triumphed by preventing the Confederates from recapturing Nashville. While on a visit from Wales in 1865, a correspondent named John Griffith who wrote for the weekly newspaper *Y Faner* [The Banner], managed to get an interview with the general himself:

> Cwrddais hefyd yn y ddinas hono – Nashville – a'r
> Cadfridog Thomas, Cymro ydyw o fodoliaeth, er nad yw
> yn medru siarad Cymraeg, ac yn dwyn sel fawr dros yr *hen*
> genedl. Cafodd ef ei eni yn nhalaeth Virginia; ymfudasai
> ei daid o Gymru, ac ymsefydlodd yn rhyw barth o dalaeth
> Pennsylvania. Y mae'r blaid Rhyddfrydig yn Tennessee o un
> llais dros gael Thomas i'r gadair arlywyddol nesaf; a chefnogir
> ef yn wresog gan rai newyddiaduron o gryn ddylanwad yn
> y Gogledd. Hen fachgen – pwyllus, tawel, cool, perffaith
> ddiymhongar, agos atoch, ac mor hawdd siarad ag ef ag ydyw
> ag unrhyw un o hen ffermwyr Dyffryn Clwyd yma, pwy
> bynnag yw'r hawddaf – di-bomp hollol – *The only one of our
> great generals,* ebai'r Governor Brownlow, wrth ei anerch pan
> yn cyflwyno medal aur iddo fel rhodd gan dalaeth Tennessee
> – *The only one of our great generals that committed no mistake
> during our great struggle.*

[*I also met in this city – Nashville – with General Thomas, Welsh by descent, and though unable to speak Welsh, he holds a strong attachment towards the old nation. He was born in the state of Virginia, his grandfather having emigrated from Wales, and settled in some part of Pennsylvania. The Liberal [Republican] Party in Tennessee are united in having him as the next to occupy the presidential chair; and he's warmly supported by some of the influential newspapers in the North. The old lad – cautious, quiet, cool, perfectly unostentatious, approachable, and as easy to talk to as any old farmer in the Clwyd Valley, whoever is the easiest – completely without pomp – "The only one of our great generals," said Governor Brownlow, on addressing him while presenting him with a gold medal as a gift from the state of Tennessee – "The only one of our great generals that committed no mistake during our great struggle."*]

Between his connection with Chattanooga's not too distant past and a background that extended back to one of Virginia's earlier Welsh families ("Cymro ardderchog mewn calon a theimlad" – an excellent Welshman in heart and spirit according to another report), no better could have been found for the honour being bestowed on him at the eisteddfod. The ritual of 'chairing' a bard calls for a ceremonial sword to be partially unsheathed and the audience is asked to respond and confirm that there is indeed peace in the land. An affirmative response is required for the ceremony to proceed and so here they were following a time-honoured tradition in a city where 30 years earlier General Thomas had received Grant's desperate plea: "Hold Chattanooga at all hazards. I will be there as soon as possible." And to which Thomas had replied, "We will hold the town till we starve." So for a city that had itself been under siege, the eisteddfod ceremony with its call for peace must have taken on a special significance.

Yet, despite the audience's resounding affirmative response on the three occasions a ceremonial sword was partially unsheathed and asked if there was peace ("Dadweinwyd y cledd, gofynwyd gyda dwysder a oedd heddwch, ac atebwyd mewn tair taran floedd bwysleisiol a nodweddiadol iawn"), it only served to detract from what was foremost on the minds of the many present. Given the situation regarding convict labour, these were also troublesome times and, by the following week, in the 6 November issue of *The Chattanooga Times*, word had leaked out of how a less publicized meeting had taken place to determine a course of action that had all the potential of leading to a military confrontation:

> During the meeting of the Welsh Eisteddfod in Chattanooga on the memorable Friday, a secret meeting was held by the miners present, and the convict question discussed. It now transpires that the action of the Briceville men was endorsed, and Tracy City and Whitwell given to understand that they would receive all necessary assistance.
>
> The members from Alabama and Georgia were eager for instructions, and an elaborate plan to release all the convicts at Pratt mines [Alabama] was discussed. It was decided that as soon as Tennessee was rid of convict miners, Alabama men would be assisted in reducing the stockade and prison at Pratt mines. Georgia was to be the last on the string, because only two mines in Georgia work convicts, the remainder being free labour.
>
> The danger particularly dwelt upon by the Alabama miners was the proximity of Birmingham to Pratt mines, and it was feared that assistance would reach the guards and prison authorities before the release could be effected. The Briceville men did not consider that a drawback and held Knoxville up as an example saying that the citizens openly approved of their actions and gave them all assistance in their power, even supplying them with arms and ammunitions of war.

The above account shows that not only were the Welsh deeply committed to the struggle against convict labour but they had managed to turn one of their most cherished cultural festivals into a hotbed of political intrigue.

Industrial and Cultural Leadership

Recruitment of Workers

In a conference paper on 'Networking among Welsh Industrial Immigrants' and then elaborated on in his later 2008 book, *Welsh Americans: A History of Assimilation in the Coalfields*, Ronald L Lewis of West Virginia University draws attention to the influence that certain Pennsylvanian mining superintendents had when it came to attracting skilled workers from Wales. By the time Tennessee experienced its industrial growth, it was more of a case of persuading those already in Pennsylvania to cast their sights further south. From his earlier experiences in Lauden, it was John H Jones who had enticed Joseph Richards to take such a step, and given the latter's popularity with the mill workers of Danville, Pennsylvania, the opportunity of working under his supervision once more would have appealed to many.

About the only Welsh mine operator of note who did not work in Pennsylvania prior to coming to Tennessee was Evan J Davies of the East Tennessee Coal Co. Making his situation even more unusual was the fact that he had no previous experience in either the iron or coal industry. Yet his name appears amongst the five Welshmen who were singled out for having made a significant contribution to the area's advancement:

Bydd ef [Evan J Davies], y ddau Richards, sef Joseph a David,
Abraham Lloyd, Soddy, a James T Williams, Chattanooga, yn
cael eu cofio yn y dyfodol fel rhai a gymerasant ran bwysig yn
nechreuad datblygiad adnoddau glofaol y rhanbarth.

[*He (Evan J Davies), the two Richards, viz., Joseph and David,
Abraham Lloyd, Soddy, and James T Williams, Chattanooga will
be remembered in future as those who played an important part in the
initial development of the region's coal resources.*]

A brief examination of his background reveals why he lacked
the wealth of experience possessed by those co-named with him.
At an early age he had left his home area of Llandysul for the larger
market town of Carmarthen and there he managed to pursue
an apprenticeship as a stonemason. After emigrating in 1870, he
spent a year in Ohio before moving south, first to Chattanooga
and then on to Knoxville. Under construction at the time was a
fairly large government building and, for almost three years, he
toiled in providing it with its roof. This he accomplished using
slate rather than the customary wooden shingles as until that time
slate had been considered inappropriate for the warmer southern
climate. His success enabled him to start his own construction
company, and this proved to be highly successful. He continued
with its operation until deciding on a different course in 1876.
With his new-found managerial skills, he became associated with
a group of miners who were about to open their own coalmine in
Caryville, Tennessee. Although this effort was to fail, it eventually
led him to becoming president of the East Tennessee Coal Co.,
with its mining operation in Dowlais, Kentucky and its main
office in Knoxville. As he was a relatively unknown in the Welsh
mining community in Pennsylvania, one can only presume that it
was the initial few miners from Mahanoy City who had enticed
their co-workers to follow. Between the company's success
under his leadership and his eagerness to help out with different
Welsh activities, it's no wonder that he was once described as "a

rich gentleman and one of the more warm-hearted Welshmen we have in this country" [boneddwr cyfoethog ac un o'r Cymry mwyaf twymgalon feddwn yn y wlad].

As influential as any of the five singled out for their significant contributions was Joseph Richards. Above all, it was his expertise that had ensured the commercial success of the mill in Knoxville. His own introduction to working in the mills had come by way of Hirwaun, where his parents had settled (the father was originally from Tyddyn-y-Garreg, Cydweli and the mother from Llanarthie). After a period at the well-known Cyfartha Works, he moved to Cwmafon where he also got married. By 1840 he was ready for yet another move, this time to Danville, the Pennsylvania town where Joseph Parry's family, who were related to him, would settle 14 years later. There he remained for twenty years, having become a superintendent over the last five. His popularity amongst the workers was unsurpassed and on his departure they took the unusual step of presenting him with a gold cup with the following inscription engraved on it: "Presented to Joseph Richards by the workmen of the Rough & Ready Mills, Danville, Pa., August 2nd, 1860." Such deep-felt sentiments suggest that many of them would have welcomed the opportunity of working under his guidance once again.

Also to contribute towards the prosperity of Knoxville was his brother, David Richards. After gaining familiarity with the iron mills, first at the Pendaren Works and then in the Rhymni, he followed his brother to Danville in 1845. Not long afterwards he had the misfortune of losing his wife and on remarrying in 1849, it was to a sister of the Thomas D Lewis who later ran the Knoxville Ice Co. (This company was not started until 1876 and in its heyday it supplied the residents of Knoxville with up to 13 tons of ice daily.) David Richards would remain in Danville for a total of 19 years and, as with his brother, he was also chosen to become a superintendent. In common with the vast majority of the Welsh immigrants, he had become a staunch Republican over the years, and in the period leading up to Lincoln's reelection, he and an individual named W D Kelly had taken it upon themselves to make stump speeches on his behalf. So widespread was their fame in the industrial heartland of Pennsylvania that they were often referred to as Pig Iron Kelly and Blair County Puddler (see the appendix of this chapter about his visit to the Ford Theatre).

From its very beginning he had been involved with the Knoxville Iron and Coal Co. and after his brother's departure for Chattanooga, it appears that he was the one chosen to oversee the mill's operation. In the mid 1870s he vehemently opposed the introduction of convict labour at the company's mine in Coal Creek. This resulted in him having to leave Knoxville for a period, his moral stance having hurt him financially as well: "sticking to such principles has cost him some thousands of dollars" [y mae sefyll at yr egwyddor hon wedi costio iddo rhai miloedd o ddoleri].

His place of temporary exile was Lynchburg in the south-western part of Virginia, and in the process of being organized there at the time was a company that later became to be known as the Glamorgan Pipe Works. Named after Wales's most industrialized county, one can only speculate as to whether this was the company he became associated with and if the same sort of 'networking' as proposed by Ron L Lewis of West Virginia University had led him there. At one period this company was renowned for the artistic design of its fire hydrants.

On turning one's attention to Soddy, one can safely assume that it was Abraham Lloyd, above all others, who was responsible for making the mining operation such a prominent enterprise: "It is him primarily that Soddy can thank for its existence" [iddo ef yn bennaf y mae Soddy i ddiolch am ei bodolaeth]. Born in Pontfaen, Glamorgan in 1845, he had worked in Aberdare until he left for America as an 18 year-old in 1863. A year later he married a Welsh girl in Pittsburgh, and in November 1866 he joined a newly-formed Welsh company located in Brookfield, Ohio. This led to his coming to Soddy where he eventually became the principal owner of the Soddy Coal Co. He also managed to start another three mines in Arkansas, spending up to six years there before returning to Soddy in 1891. Such was his inspirational leadership that his associates could proclaim "he is both mayor and king of Soddy" [efe yw maer a brenin Soddy].

Working in conjunction with him over the years was a James T Williams, the last of the five to be singled out for their leadership. He had been born in the vicinity of St Clears, Carmarthenshire, and at a place that is incorrectly spelt as Mydrim on his headstone. He left there at a relatively young age to find work in Aberdare, and eight years after emigrating in 1860, he got married to Mary Ann Davies. He had worked at Soddy from almost its infancy and later, when the majority of the investors became disillusioned with the Cincinnati Southern Railroad's failure to provide a railroad link in a timely manner, it was left to him and Abraham Lloyd to buy out their stake in the mine. While still at Soddy, and before relocating to Chattanooga to take care of the company's marketing interests, he had served as supervisor to Soddy's Sunday school. In a short note that appeared in the *Knoxville Sentinel* on 13 August 1891, he is referred to as Alderman James T Williams. At that particular time he was making his way back to Chattanooga after visiting some additional mines he owned in Coal Creek. In the same short account he was referred to as "a prominent coal operator" and when it came to the Chattanooga Eisteddfod of 1891, it was him that they would honour through having him serve as its honorary president.

Above all others these five were the ones who created the opportunities for others to follow. Also instrumental when it came to attracting experienced workers would be the advanced publicity associated with the so-called eisteddfodau. Not only did they signify which areas of the country had a significant Welsh population, but also where others with compatible skills could conceivably find work.

Family ties would also play a prominent part when it came to relocating and this appears to have been exceptionally strong in the case of Knoxville. Related to the three Richards brothers were not only the two close associates who ran the company's machine shop and mining operations, but a whole host of cousins. The Margaret Davies who had once taken care of the boarding house in Coal Creek was said to be a sister to both the Richardses father and Elizabeth Parry, Joseph Parry's mother. These sisters, as well as the parents of the Richardses, would eventually follow their siblings to Knoxville. Also to make their homes here were three of Margaret Davies's children. As to the Joseph Parry who was to become Wales's foremost music composer, two of his sisters, Jane and Betsey, were recognized for their singing abilities and one or other of them was the so-called "singer of great renown" who entertained the Welsh community in Knoxville.

Related to them all were the various members of the Price family whose mother was said to be an aunt to the music composer Joseph Parry. Both of the Price parents were Welsh born, the father from Cwmtwrch and the mother from Blaenafon. Their children were raised in a mining community located a few miles from Pottsville, Pennsylvania, and that had been named after the St Clears found in Wales. Two of the sons were destined to run the Knoxville Furniture Co. and when another brother, Dr Levi Jones Price, arrived in Knoxville in 1871, there to greet him in addition to the brothers was a sister as well. Despite his brothers' good fortune, he still needed a scholarship to attend what was already a well-established medical school in Louisville, Kentucky. He did so after a brief period of employment at the foundry's offices in Coal Creek as well as at Knoxville. He graduated in 1877 and, on gaining experience in places as diverse as Pennsylvania and Texas and that included a limited period in Coal Creek, he eventually set up his own practice in Knoxville.

So, largely as a result of family ties, Knoxville had stood to benefit from a variety of productive relatives, ranging from the Richards brothers who had led the foundry into becoming Knoxville's largest employer, to the Price brothers who employed another 70 to 80 workers. As to the composer Joseph Parry, and after a prolonged absence in Wales, he eventually undertook a return visit to the United States in 1898. Given the extent of his family connections in Knoxville, it comes as no surprise to find that he eagerly awaited the opportunity of reuniting with "you my cousins in Tennessee, your families, and grandchildren, after an absence of twenty-seven years!" [chwithau fy nghefndryd yn Tennessee, eich teuluoedd, a'ch wyrion, ar ôl saith mlynedd ar hugain o absenoldeb!].

From Self-Education to Integration

Whilst referring to their initial period in Knoxville, the Rev. Thomas Thomas mentions how John Jones (formerly of Lauden) had just returned from Washington after being granted a patent. He had devised a simplified way of reworking old rails without having to cut them up. During the latter part of the nineteenth century, his counterparts in Pennsylvania would receive numerous patents, from producing firebricks that could withstand high temperatures while exhibiting minimal expansion, to furnaces adapted for warming trains. The so-called 'Jones Mixer' was named after another of the numerous Joneses, the William Richard Jones previously referred to as having briefly worked in Chattanooga prior to the Civil War.

Denied the benefit of a formal education, such individuals often developed their desire for self-improvement through attending and participating in literary societies, such as the one found in Coal Creek, and also the eisteddfodau. Then there were the Sunday schools, and here the adult classes received as much emphasis as those arranged for children. Once a year they would collectively subject themselves to an oral exam conducted by a guest minister, and it was up to him to challenge their understanding of a predesignated Biblical text. Between such activities many would become acquainted with not only the scriptures but a variety of the broader issues of the day. Included amongst what was published in the Welsh language, and having been available to them in Pennsylvania during the period leading up to the 1860 Presidential election, were two 16-page pamphlets supportive of Lincoln's campaign. These appeared at a time when Lincoln was still considered a rank outsider. Their content differed greatly; the one published in Pottsville, Pennsylvania being based primarily on the Lincoln-Douglas debates, and the one from Utica, New York on Lincoln's Cooper Institute address. So for those who were yet to master the rudiments of English, the most pertinent information when it came to assessing what Lincoln and the new Republican Party stood for was readily available to them. Additional publications, ranging from religious texts to collections of poems, continued to be published right through to the end of the century.

With the minister Iorthyn Gwynedd, as capable and as well-read as he was, even his formal education had been confined to less than a year. In more recent times his well-known *Hanes Cymry America* from 1872, which outlined the Welsh settlements of the period, has been made available in translation through the efforts of Phillips G Davies from Iowa State University. Prior to his coming to America, and during his very first ministry at Penarth Chapel, Llanfair Caereinion, Iorthyn Gwynedd had provided testimony for a government report, dating from 1847, that later became the subject of considerable controversy in Wales. Bound in three volumes under blue covers, the report came to be known as *The Treachery of the Blue Books*. What was being submitted concerning Aberdâr has already been referred to, and implied throughout the report was that all the ills and backwardness of Wales could be attributed to its language and culture. From a relatively recent talk given by a T Elgan Davies to the local community of Iorthyn Gwynedd's first ministry, it appears that he had been the only person throughout all of Wales who was courageous enough to provide testimony that reflected a Welsh perspective. His lone stance has also been discussed by Gwawr Jones in an article that appeared in the 1998 issue of the journal, *Y Cofiadur* [The Recorder].

As devastating as the Blue Books were in their day, what is even more troubling is that many of the prejudicial attitudes exhibited in them still prevail a century and a half later. Too often governmental and other institutions show very little insight as to what is required to prevent Welsh from becoming another casualty amongst the languages that are predicted to perish during the present century. Over its 100 years of existence, even the University of Wales has been a dismal failure when it comes to providing its student body with a bilingual facility which matches the percentage of Welsh speakers in general. Needed to be addressed are such prevailing attitudes as those which discourage the use of the Welsh language even when the overwhelming majority at hand prefer to converse in it. Invariably, it is the Welsh speakers who are perceived as being at fault if they don't instantaneously turn to English, and not those individuals who expect nothing less. Too often it is the unenlightened hiring polices of nationwide bus companies or supermarket chains that dictate which language prevails in every day use. Such a practice of treating the language with total disdain is not only demeaning to Welsh speakers but it also leaves them open to ridicule if their degree of fluency falls short of what it is in their native tongue. Given such lingering attitudes, Iorthyn Gwynedd's words remain as poignant as ever and it would not be out of place to display some of his sentiments, as italicized below, at the entrance of every educational institution in Wales:

> There are some people of the Welsh nation that are in the habit of speaking English with their children from their infancy, and, consequently, there are many children of the Welsh people that cannot speak their mother tongue. We consider this a very bad practice, because those children can speak no language properly, and generally cannot enjoy the privileges of our Sunday schools, because they are conducted in the Welsh language. *Every child has a right to know the language of his parents. To deprive them of that is an insult to our nation, language, and country.* We greatly abhor this practice, but it is the case generally on the borders of England, and this is one reason why Offa's Dyke is like Sodom and Galilee of the Gentiles in ungodliness and ignorance…

> *Penarth, Llanfair*
> *26 January 1847*   I have the honour to be,
>   Gentlemen,
>   Yours, very humbly,
>   Robt Dafydd Thomas

Thirty years after providing such testimony, here was Iorthyn Gwynedd in a position to observe how his fellow countrymen were excelling as industrial leaders in Tennessee without relinquishing their heritage. Still embracing their traditional culture as much as ever were all five of those singled out for their leadership. The first recorded account of an eisteddfod being held in Wales dates back to 1176, and encouraging them to maintain that tradition in Tennessee was E J Davies of the East Tennessee Coal Co.: "he above all is the one that needs to be thanked for the first eisteddfod held in the South, viz., the Knoxville Eisteddfod of 1890" [iddo ef yn bennaf y rhaid diolch am yr Eisteddfod gyntaf a gynhaliwyd yn y De, sef Eisteddfod Knoxville yn 1890]. His dedication to eisteddfodau was again matched by his generosity when it came to renovating their Knoxville church. And were it not for the extreme sacrifice of another of their Knoxville leaders, Joseph Richards, it is doubtful whether their church would have been built in the first place. Not only did he oversee its construction, but on more than one occasion he was left with having to pay the workers out of his own pocket. Then there was his brother David Richards, who, over time, became to be affectionately known as Uncle Dave. Not only did he participate in the activities of the church and the Welsh society, but he also devoted much of his time to aid the city's poor. As to the James T Williams who later moved to Chattanooga from Soddy, he had managed to raise all six of his children through the medium of Welsh.

Also to be found in Knoxville were relatives of several others back in Wales who, as with Iorthyn Gwynedd, had been instrumental in the struggle to retain their heritage. Already mentioned in this regard was Wales's first non-Anglican Member of Parliament, Henry Richard, who not only helped promote the formation of the United Nations's forerunner, but also did as much as anybody to nullify the negative image of Wales fostered by the Blue Books. Then there was the celebrated Thomas Levi, the only one of five brothers who didn't leave for the greener pastures of the United States.

The youngest brother, Dr Joseph Levi, had left Wales in 1851 and was later married to Betsey Richards, another sister of the Richardses. Up until his untimely death in 1874 he had practiced in Knoxville, attending Iorthyn Gwynedd's wife during her terminal illness. More so than anybody else, he had helped Iorthyn Gwynedd overcome his enormous sense of grief of being away in Wales at the time of her death. Left behind in Wales was Thomas Levi who, as an eight year-old in 1823, had been given a taste of what it was like to work in the iron mills. On becoming a Methodist preacher and through his numerous publications, he would become a household name in Wales. At one stage he even collaborated with Joseph Parry on a composition called 'Cantata yr Adar' [Cantata of the Birds].

As important as any of his endeavours was his monthly magazine *Trysorfa'r Plant* [Children's Treasury], which provided the youth of Wales with reading material in their own language for the first time. Such was the impact of this highly-acclaimed magazine that it earned him the distinction of being referred to as the 'Children's Apostle'. As the founding editor he managed to persuade at least one distant brother to contribute towards its content. Appearing in the September 1873 issue of *Trysorfa'r Plant* was an article that gave the children of Wales a taste of what it was like to live in Knoxville. Under the heading 'Llythyr at Tommy Bach' [A letter to little Tommy], it was written in the form of a letter directed at a six year-old:

Yr oedd yn *Bedwerydd o Orffenaf* yma ddoe – Dydd Gŵyl fawr America. Yr wyt ti yn o ieuanc i ddeall ei hystyr – sef cadw mewn cof sefydliad ein llywodraeth; ond pe buaset yma, ni fuaset yn rhy ieuanc i fwynhau y rhialtwch oedd yma ar y diwrnod. Yr oedd y bobl yn myned allan yn dyrfaoedd i'r coed a'r meusydd, i yfed te, bwyta teisenau, *tarts, ice-cream,* a ffrwythau, chwareu, saethu, *swingo,* a phob peth i ymddyfyru.

Bum i allan gyda thyrfa o Gymry mewn coedwig fawr, ddwy neu dair milltir o'r dref; ac yr oedd yno ugeiniau o blant bach Cymreig, yn gallu siarad Cymraeg fel tithau, wedi gwysgo yn grand – yn fechgyn a merched. Yr oedd yno y *siglihois* (swings) mwyaf a welais erioed, a'r plant yn codi arnynt cuwch a phen y ty. Yr oedd yn fyd braf ar y plant, yn cael eu gwala o redeg, neidio, chwareu *rings, Copenhagen,* canu, adrodd ac areithio. Diwrnod mawr iawn ydoedd, a buasai Tomi bach wrth fodd ei galon i fod yn eu mysg.

[It was the Fourth of July *here yesterday – America's great holiday. You are on the young side to understand its significance – viz., to keep in memory the establishment of our government; but had you been here, you wouldn't have been too young to enjoy the festivity of the*

day. Great crowds of people were going out to the woods and fields, to drink tea, eat cakes, tarts, ice-cream, and fruits, to play, shoot, swing and everything that provides enjoyment.

Along with many of the Welsh I went out to a great forest, two or three miles from the town, and there were scores of Welsh-oriented children, able to speak Welsh just like you, having been dressed in a grand manner – boys and girls. Here were the largest siglihois *(swings) I ever saw, with the children getting as high as the tops of houses. It was a great time for the children, having their fill of running, jumping, playing rings, Copenhagen, singing, reciting, and giving speeches. It was a great day, and little Tommy would have enjoyed immensely being there in their midst.*]

From the above description it becomes apparent that they had managed to arrange social gatherings in Knoxville well before the emergence of the Cymdeithas Gymrodorol Knoxville (Welsh Society of Knoxville) in 1891. Another more somber part of the same letter goes on to explain what had transpired in the city's not too distant past and how the slaves had finally been freed:

Y maent yn awr yn rhydd i gyd; nis gall neb eu prynu, na'u gwerthu, na'u chwipio. Bu rhyfel mawr iawn yma, er mwyn gorfodi y dynion i'w gollwng yn rhydd. Bu ymladd dychrynllyd yn y man yr wyf fi yn ysgrifennu y llythyr hwn. Mae yr hen gloddiau mawr i fyny yma yn awr, lle yr oedd y *cannons* wedi eu gosod, lle yr oedd y milwyr yn cysgodi eu hunain, tra yn saethu y dynion oedd yn dyfod yn eu herbyn. Chwalwyd y rhan fwyaf o'r tai oedd yn y dref o'r pryd hwnnw; ac y mae tyllau y bwledi i'w gweled yn awr yn yr ychydig sydd wedi eu gadael i fyny... Ond, fe enillwyd y dydd o blaid y bobl dduon, druain, ac fe'u gollyngwyd i gyd yn rhydd. Mae yma luoedd ohonynt o hyd, ond chaiff neb eu prynu a'u gwerthu yn awr; cânt fyned a dyfod yn awr fel y mynent, a derbyn cyflog am eu gwaith. Mae un ohonynt – Hannah – yn eistedd yn y ty gyda mi yn awr, yr hon sydd yn byw yn seler y ty hwn, a'i gwyneb mor ddu a'r glo; mae wedi rhoddi ei llun hi a'i gwr i mi, i'w ddwyn drosodd i'r hen wlad.

[*They are now all free; nobody can buy them, or sell them or whip them. There was a great war here, so that everybody would be forced to set them free. There was terrible fighting around the spot where I write this letter. The old earth works are still up, where the cannons had been placed, and where the soldiers sought cover while shooting at those who came towards them. At that time most of the houses in the town were torn to shreds; and bullet holes can still be seen in the few houses that have been left to stand... but the day was won on behalf of the black people, pitiful as they were, and all of them were set free. There are lots of them still here, but by now nobody is allowed to sell or buy them; they can come and go as they please, and receive a wage for their work. One of them – Hannah – is sitting in the house with me now, she lives in the basement of this very house, and her face is as black as coal; she has given me a picture of her husband and herself to bring over to the old country.*]

Following Thomas Levi's example a number of children-orientated magazines started to appear within the United States, the most notable being the one published out of Utica, New York over the period 1872–5. Known as *Blodau'r Oes* [Flowers of the Age], it was meant to appeal to the children being raised in such communities as the one found in Knoxville's Mechanicsville district. But as would invariably happen with all ethnic groups, the language would be gone within a generation or two. In Knoxville this is reflected by their failure to sustain their once cherished church by the beginning of the twentieth century.

For many of the Welsh immigrants it appears that they could judiciously balance what it took to retain their distinctive culture while yet becoming accepted as Americans. In many ways America was as close as they could get to the idealism they continued to yearn for in Wales itself. No longer having to contend with former injustices, the main impact on the newly arrived from Wales would be the loss of any affinity they might have once held for being 'British'. Suggestive of such a transition, as well as to how readily they gained acceptance in their adopted country, are the following comments which appeared in the monthly *Y Cenhadwr Americanaidd* in 1840. Written by a minister from Pittsburgh, who wrote under the bardic name of Iorwerth, he would have been aquainted with many of the first wave of Welsh industrial workers to arrive in Pennsylvania:

> Un o'r pethau hyfrydaf mewn modd gwladol yw rhyddid, yr hyn sydd yn gwneud mawr wahaniaeth rhwng y wlad hon a gwlad ein genedigaeth... pan oedd rhyw etholiad gwladol yng Nghymru yr oedd yn rhaid i'r deiliad roi ei bleidlais gyda ei feistr, neu fod mewn perygl o golli ei dir... mae hynawsedd yr Americaniaid tuag atom ni fel cenedl yn galw arnom ninau i ddangos iddynt mai cyfeillion iddynt ydym ninnau... mae lles personol pob Cymro yn ei gymell ef i wneud ei hun yn ddinasydd yn ddioed.
>
> [*From a governmental perspective one of the more delightful things is freedom, which makes a huge difference between this country and the land of our birth... When there was some political election in Wales, the tenant had to place his vote with his master, or face the danger of losing his land... The friendliness of the Americans towards us as a nation calls on us to show that we are their friends too... The advantages on a personal level beckons every Welshman to make himself a citizen without delay.*]

In Knoxville and as elsewhere in the country, they managed to integrate without much difficulty. Noted all along for their singing, it isn't that surprising to find that a son of the third of the Richardses brothers came to be recognized as a leading baritone in Knoxville. Instead of just taking part in Welsh-oriented events, others of similar background would find a wider audience by singing mining ballads. In his introduction to a collection of such songs, *Coal Dust on the Fiddle*, George Korson acknowledges how many of the participants had branched away from the eisteddfodau of the older generation. Also indicative of their ability to integrate with relative ease is how one of their descendants was selected to represent the United States at the Olympics. Another emerged as one of Knoxville's finest surgeons and, in Atlanta, they provided one of its medical schools with its dean. Then referred to by Will Thomas Hale and Dixon L Merritt in Volume 6 of their *A History of Tennessee and Tennesseans*, are the accomplishments of Thomas Rees Price (Knoxville Furniture Co.). Even though he was part of the first generation to arrive, it illustrates how he, like many others, was well on the way to becoming an integral part of the city:

> For upwards of thirty-five years Thomas Rees Price was identified with the commercial and industrial activities of Knoxville, contributing to the city's material progress and prosperity to an extent equalled by few of his contemporaries. He was not only an important factor in various lines of business, but also in social and civic development. He contributed by his personal activities to the advancement and general welfare, and was one of the citizens who helped maintain a high level of public spirit and moral and social justice in this community... Though in later years he was regarded as one of the most prosperous citizens of Knoxville, [he] had begun his career a poor boy, and had relied upon the skill of his hands and the alleged ability of his business judgement to advance him from one place to another in business life. In later years his name had a variety of associations with the business community, such as probably no other Knoxville citizen possessed.

As attached as they were to their own cultural background, it never kept them isolated from others. As already seen, they could celebrate 4 July with just as much vigour as anybody else, and wherever they settled they usually managed to contribute to the community at large. In 1911 this became the subject of an editorial that appeared in one of the more admired Kansas newspapers, the *Emporia Gazette*. The paper's owner, William Allen White, was generally considered as being one of the country's foremost nineteenth-century editors, and amongst his acquaintances were the likes of President Roosevelt and the novelist Dean Howells. Thriving in Emporia at the time were as many as five Welsh-language churches, and when his paper reported on how their Second Presbyterian Church had managed to build a new home for their minister, he took the opportunity to comment on the city's Welsh:

> The Welsh people of this community have lived here for over a generation. They have been the best single strain of blood in our Emporia life. They have Americanized, but have retained their strong qualities of thrift, of honesty, of industry, of deep moral qualities. Also they are the basis of the best artistic feeling in the community. More than the Americans of several generations, these newer Americans have the sense that money is not all of life, that there is something better than hard cash, and they have given Emporia much of its best tone, its steady-going homely purpose and its wholesome details.

Also being published in Emporia was a Welsh weekly newspaper known as *Colomen Columbia* [Columbian Dove]. As already alluded to, much of what can be gleaned about their accomplishments in Tennessee and Kentucky is derived from a series of articles that appeared in it, starting with its 14 April 1892 issue. They were submitted by an individual who wrote under the name of 'Bonllwyn', which literally means the 'base of a bush' (a place so-named is to be found near Rhydaman in south Wales). As his true identity was not revealed, one can only speculate as to who he might have been. One possible candidate could be the Richard Bowen from the Powell Iron Co. who took pride in writing essays for eisteddfod competitions. However, his place of residence was Chattanooga, and somehow one gets the feeling that the writer in question might have been more familiar with Knoxville. This brings up another possibility in Howell Davies of Coal Creek, and while his winning poem at the Dowlais Eisteddfod is not particularly noteworthy, it does show that he possessed an adequate command of the written language as well as being well versed in matters pertaining to Wales. The most likely candidate however is a Rhys T Williams who had been born in the vicinity of Ystradgynlais in 1849 and had left Wales for Pennsylvania in 1882. Prior to his departure, and under a variety of assumed names, he had become a popular columnist for such publications as *Y Gwladgarwr* [The Patriot] and *Y Fellten* [The Lightning]. In 1891, a year prior to the appearance of the sequence of Tennessee related articles, he had moved to Jellico on being offered a position as secretary to some of the area's mining companies.

Whatever the writer's true identity, one reader found reason to criticize him, and that for what was considered to be a tendency to utilize too many obscure words for easy comprehension. While Bonllwyn was prepared to concede that there might be some validity to the criticism, his advice to his critic was that he should buy himself a good dictionary. Despite everything, one can presume that the writer's wide circle of acquaintances would have been delighted with what he wrote and would have willingly subscribed to the paper despite it being published from as far away as Kansas.

As informitive as this particular paper was, their reading habits were not limited to such material and often residing within a community would be someone or other who possessed a fairly extensive library. This was the first thing to be mentioned on bringing up the name of a John Williams, initially from Pencader in Wales, but who had become the 'outside superintendent' for the East Tennessee Coal Co. in Dowlais: "apart from Iorthyn Gwynedd he has the best Welsh library I've seen in the country. He possesses many of the most important Welsh books and has made much use of them" [gydag ef ag eithrio Iorthyn Gwynedd y mae y llyfrgell Gymraeg oreu a welais yn y wlad. Medda amryw o'r prif lyfrau Cymreig; ac y mae wedi gwneud llawer o ddefnydd ohonynt]. So in both Dowlais and Knoxville there was the possibility of borrowing the odd title from such collections.

In this respect Coal Creek was not to be outdone and of interest here is the ownership of the books donated to Harvard's prestigious Widener Library. The first indication as to who this might have been came from one of the activities arranged in May 2002 to commemorate the tragic loss of lives at the Fraterville mine a hundred years earlier. Apart from the memorial service held in the church built by the Welsh in Briceville, a historical tour was arranged for the benefit of the local school's fifth grade class by Barry Thacker, president of Geo/Environmental Associates in Knoxville. By chance they came across the grave of Rees R Thomas, not in Coal Creek's Welsh cemetery, but in that of the Wiley family who were once the area's dominant landowners. Two years later, and through the good grace of Barry Thacker, an opportunity arose to view the headstone. In a long-neglected cemetery that is only approachable on scrambling up a mountainside through thick overgrowth, one finds his headstone lying on its back and partly covered by the surrounding overgrowth. Alongside, and protruding no more than six inches above the ground, were two much smaller headstones that were only revealed on carefully separating a thick covering of poison ivy. They marked the burial place of two young girls, Gladys Thomas, 27 October 1886 – 7 May 1887 and Josephine Thomas, 13 January 1890 – 7 September 1891, but no indication is given as to their relationship, if any, to Rees R Thomas. His own headstone revealed that he and his wife were from Carmarthen, that he was born in 1814 and had died in 1891. From these dates one can infer that he would have been at least into his fifties when he first came to Coal Creek and that his longevity would have allowed him to witness how some of his colleagues were becoming increasingly involved with mining activities in the Jellico area.

Still in the possession of a descendant of his is a Welsh Bible published in 1804 and that had been given to Rees R Thomas by his mother in 1834. Stated in it was how he had been christened at Llanllwch Church, which is on the outskirts of Carmarthen, and a reconfirmation that his year of birth was indeed 1814. Another entry brings up the name of David R Thomas, whose year of birth is given as 1838. He was to marry Prudence Levi, a daughter of Dr Joseph Levi and Betsey Richards, and one can only speculate as to whether she had helped her father with his contribution to the children's magazine, *Trysorfa'r Plant*. As to David R Thomas himself, and being that one of the family's books in Harvard's possession was not published until 1896, which is five years after his father's death, one can surmise that he had continued to add to the collection. Not only does his name appear as a subscriber in another book published somewhat later, but it reveals that he had taken on the assumed bardic name of Gwalch Gwalia (Welsh Rascal). It is also of interest to note that another book in the family collection, a 744-page volume by Samuel Roberts entitled *Pregethau a Darlithiau* [Sermons and Lectures], had been published out of Utica, New York in 1865. At that time the author was still struggling with his Brynyffynon settlement in Tennessee.

Having survived as a result of being inserted within the covers of the family Bible, a few other brief items cast further light on the family. First, there is a three-page elegy to the Rev. Methusalem Jones of Bethesda Church in Merthyr, who had died as a 71 year-old in 1839, and well-short of his Biblical namesake. Then there is what is described as a 'canmol-gan' (praise-song) to a John Jenkins who had been an influential member of the same church for 42 years. These items tend to suggest that Rees Thomas had moved to Merthyr at one stage, where the employment opportunities would have been more forthcoming than in the vicinity of Carmarthen. This is confirmed by a more recently found obituary note in which it is stated that he had led the singing when the Bethesda Church was under the pastorship of the above mentioned Methusalem Jones. His son appears to have inherited his passion for music and still extant are the words he wrote for the hymn 'Fel yr Wyf' [As I am]. Though matching some of the phrasing of a Welsh hymn that goes by the same name, it bears little resemblance to the English hymn 'Just as I am'.

Also preserved within the Bible are a couple of handwritten items, the first being a list of ten questions which were meant as a Sunday school exercise for younger children, e. g., 'To whom did God reveal the Ten Commandments' [Wrth bwy y llefarodd Duw y Deg Gorchymun]. Then under the heading of 'Rheolau Ysgol Sabothol y MC yn Wheathersfield' [Sunday school regulations of the Methodists in Weathersfield], another handwritten note sets out a list of 20 procedural items. A brief account from *Y Drych* [The Mirror] in 1890 confirms the existence of such a church in eastern Ohio. This account appeared one year prior to Rees R Thomas's death and by then the Weathersfield Church was also nearing its final days:

> Mae ardal Weathersfield bron marw o ddarfodedigaeth gweithfaol am fod y glo wedi ei weithio allan, er fod yno eto amryw o Gymry parchus yn byw, ac eglwys wan gan y MC. Mae capel y Bedyddwyr wedi ei gau.

> [*The district of Weathersfield is nearly dead from the industrial depletion brought about by the coal being worked out. This being so despite some quite respectable Welsh persons still living there, with a Methodist Church that is not too flourishing. The Baptist Church is already closed.*]

Census records confirm that the family had once lived in Weathersfield, Ohio. By the time of the Fraterville Mine disaster in 1902, the son David R Thomas was well into his sixties but had worked in that very mine until somewhat earlier in the year.

He continued to live in Coal Creek and, one month prior to the explosion, he had inspected the mine on behalf of an insurance company. Testifying at the inquiry, he opened his remarks by stating: "I started to work in the mines when my daddy carried me on his back... "

As to the family's former books, a considerable number have by now been made available to all through being scanned as part of Google Books. One of the titles, a Biblical-based play, *Mordecai a Harman*, was recently put to good use by a Harvard student. Written in its entirety in free verse and published in Scranton, Pennsylvania in 1869, it became the basis of a study that warranted inclusion in the scholarly publication, *American Babel* (edited by Prof. Marc Shell and published by Harvard University Press in 2002). What better legacy to a self-educated mining family who had helped pioneer Tennessee's industrial development.

A hymn by David R Thomas, Coal Creek, Tennessee

FEL YR WYF

Mi nesaf at dy orsedd,
   Fel yr wyf, &c.,
Cyflawnydd aml drosedd,
   Fel yr wyf;
Hen orsedd dy drugaredd,
Mae ynddi ddwyfol fawredd
I roddi pob ymgeledd,
   Fel yr wyf, &c.,
I mi pan yn fy ngwaeledd,
   Fel yr wyf.

Ar ymchwydd mor o drallod,
   Fel yr wyf, &c.,
Bron suddo gan fy mechod,
   Fel yr wyf;
A deddf fy Nuw, "na phecha"
Yn gwaeddi am fy nifa,
Ond gwelaf lwyr ddiangfa,
   Fel yr wyf, &c.,
Drwy aberth mawr Calfaria,
   Fel yr wyf.

Erglyw o Dduw fy ngweddi,
   Fel yr wyf, &c.,
Er nad wyf yn ei haeddu,
   Fel yr wyf;
'Rho gariad im' dy foli,
Ac hefyd dy was'naethu,
Na ad fi yn fy mryntni,
   Fel yr wyf, &c.,
Gwna fi yn un o'th deulu,
   Fel yr wyf.

A visit to the Ford Theatre

A century and a half onwards it is gratifying to find that present day descendants of David Richards still refer to his son, their grandfather, in the most Welsh of ways, as "Dai John" (Dai, an abbreviated form of Dafydd or David and pronounced as the English 'die'). Well before his eventual marriage to one of Iorthyn Gwynedd's daughters, and while still a schoolboy in Pennsylvania, his father had promised him that, on doing well in his school's exams, he could accompany him to Washington and meet Lincoln in person. This probably would have transpired had Lincoln not been tied up in a cabinet meeting prompted by Grant's return at the conclusion of the Civil War. Not to be outdone and, on learning that the President would be at the Ford Theatre that evening, Dai John suggested that perhaps they could at least see him there. His father readily agreed, "I guess this will be our only chance to see him, Dai." So, present on that fateful evening was the young schoolboy Dai John who would later recall the thrill of just being present:

We sat about the center of the auditorium. It was the first time for either Father or myself to be in a regular up-to-date theatre building. It is not necessary for me to state that but for a time I was all eyes, taking in what appeared to be 'fairy land' to me. I looked about me, seeing the ground floor, the galleries, the stage, but especially the boxes on either side of the stage. I noticed the first row of boxes with a partition between, making two boxes which were on a level with the floor of the stage, then above this on the right, there was another box, the partition had been removed from this, turning the two boxes into one. The extra decorations was a notice that this was to be the President's box…

It was about 8.22 p.m. when a signal was given from the front to the orchestra leader, of the arrival of the President and party. The Orchestra at once played 'Hail to the Chief', and as the party entered, the audience rose to their feet. We did too. Then on looking to the right we saw Mr and Mrs Lincoln, Major Rathbone, and several plain clothes men, coming in and going toward the special box… Mr Lincoln appeared at the front of the box with his old stove-pipe hat placed on his left breast, when he bowed to the left, center, and right, then took his seat, and the play continued…

The performance had gotten under way at 8 p.m., and until the President's arrival twenty minutes later, the audience had not been particularly attentive, many fearing that they had missed the opportunity of seeing him after all. Shortly after ten o'clock things came to an abrupt halt on stage and, to Dai John, amongst others, it appeared as if a member of the cast had missed a cue. This unexpected pause provided the well-known actor John Wilkes Booth with an opportunity to approach the President, possibly under the assumption that he was about to express regret over the delay. What was about to transpire went completely unnoticed by the audience and, shortly afterwards, when John Wilkes Booth emerged on stage, his sudden and unexpected appearance was greeted by prolonged applause. Most of the audience remained completely oblivious as to what had actually happened until a surgeon seated towards the back was approached for assistance. On overhearing the request, the person in the adjacent seat stood up on his chair and bellowed out that the President had been shot.

Many years were to go by before Dai John came to realize that it was not a missed cue that had brought about the fatal interruption in the performance. On leaving her dressing room an actress named Catherine Evans had the misfortune of having her dress caught on a nail and, not wanting to appear on stage in a torn dress, had insisted on having it sown up first. At the time of his own death in 1932, Dai John had outlived all those present on that fateful evening. His comment regarding how he had witnessed Lincoln being escorted into the theatre by not only Major Rathbone, but by "several plain clothes men" casts doubt on the general belief that Lincoln had been left completely unprotected. Also vivid on Dai John's mind was how, earlier in the day, he had witnessed Washington at its most exhilarating, with bands marking the end of the war by playing everywhere, and complete strangers embracing each other on the streets. As to the Cabinet meeting which had prevented him from being introduced to Lincoln in person, the *New York Times* saw it as one of the defining moments in the country's history:

At 11 o'clock the Cabinet and Gen. Grant met with him [Lincoln], and in one of the most satisfactory and important Cabinet meetings held since the first inauguration, the future policy of the Administration was harmoniously and unanimously agreed on. When it adjourned, Secretary Stanton said he felt that the government was stronger than at any previous period since the rebellion commenced.

The Coal Creek Watershed Foundation

Founded in 2000 by Barry Thacker, President of Geo/ Environmental Associates in Knoxville, its objective being to help "improve the quality of life in the Coal Creek Watershed", an area that was no longer as affluent as it had once been. The foundation's main effort to date has centred around motivating and providing financial assistance for local children to go to college. According to Barry Thacker:

Coal Creek students at Lake City Middle School and Anderson County High School complete community service projects, including installation of historical markers to educate others about local history. Four of the historic sites: Briceville Church, Fraterville Miners' Circle, Cross Mountain Miners' Circle and Fort Anderson on Militia Hill are listed on the National Register of Historic Places. Participation in these projects qualifies them for the Nantglo Scholarship, which provides financial assistance for them to attend college.

Nantglo is Welsh for Coal Creek and 29 Coal Creek students have received scholarships totalling $202,500. The Welsh miners serve as great role models for Coal Creek students. They fuelled the industrial revolution, abolished the convict lease system in Tennessee, made working conditions safer for future miners, and still found time to preserve and celebrate their heritage.

In 2003 Barry Thacker's achievements were recognized through his selection as the 61st recipient of the prestigious Hoover Medal. The citation reads:

For successfully applying his engineering judgement, skill, and ingenuity to meet the social, physical, educational, and environmental needs of the Appalachian Coal Creek Watershed.

Past recipients include Dwight D Eisenhower (in 1960) and Jimmy Carter (in 1998). Amongst those invited by Barry Thacker to address students at the Briceville Elementary School was Dr John Kesterson, a retired surgeon from Knoxville who was to elaborate on a genetic defect he had inherited through being Welsh:

Do you see the curled fingers on my hand? I have a genetic abnormality called Dupuytren's Contracture which is common in the Welsh. It was passed down to me through the genes of my old Welsh grandmother. She was a nurse in Coal Creek and I guess I also got my love of medicine from her. Her father, David R Thomas, was a coal miner in Coal Creek as was his father, Rees R Thomas.

One of the lessons I learned from my parents was the importance of a good education. I was fortunate to graduate from the University of Tennessee and Vanderbilt University Medical School before joining the Army as a surgeon during World War II. Getting a good education will provide opportunities for you if you also heed their advice. With that, I'll do as my grandmother suggested when she taught me the Welsh phrase that translates to 'sit down and shut your mouth', something I always have a hard time doing.

Bibliographical Notes

By far the most significant sources of information on the Welsh presence in Tennessee are the Welsh-language monthly magazines and weekly newspapers that were once published in the United States. The first successful periodical of its kind was *Y Cyfaill* [The Friend], a monthly magazine first published in 1838 which went on to serve the interests of this country's Welsh Methodists for 95 years. Not to be outdone, and two years later, the Congregational Church followed with their *Y Cenhadwr Americanaidd* [The American Missionary]. Eventually the Baptists would get into the act by starting several short-lived magazines of their own. Whenever a community fell short of what it took to sustain more than one church, the general practice was to collectively worship as a Congregational Church. As this was generally the case in Tennessee, the most likely magazine to carry articles about their presence would be *Y Cenhadwr Americanaidd*.

The most successful of the weekly newspapers was *Y Drych* [The Mirror]. First published in New York City in January 1851, it preceded the *New York Times* by nine months and remained a Welsh-language weekly until well into the twentieth century. Even though it occasionally carried an article pertaining to the Welsh presence in Tennessee, pride and place here must go to a rather obscure weekly newspaper that was initially published out of Emporia, Kansas. Known as *Colomen Columbia* [Columbian Dove], it carried a series of articles concerning their activities, ranging from the exploits of the initial pre-war few, and continuing right up to the time of publication in 1892/3.

For a more general account of the Welsh in America, see Edward G Hartmann's *Americans from Wales* which was first published in Boston in 1967. Also worthy of attention is the highly acclaimed *Hanes Cymry America* [History of the Welsh in America] which was published in Utica, New York. At the time of its publication in 1872 its author, R D Thomas, had already committed himself to becoming their pastor in Knoxville. As familiar as he would have been with the city, his observations regarding Tennessee as a whole are confined to 2½ pages. Despite such a shortcoming, his book serves to substantiate many of the more detailed accounts found elsewhere.

For a general background of the Tennessee which became their new home, one can turn to a number of texts ranging from Goodspeed's *History of Tennessee* that dates from 1886/7 to the more recently published *Encyclopaedia of Appalachia*. As to Knoxville itself, William Bruce Wheeler's book, *Knoxville Tennessee* (2005) provides a fascinating account of how the city evolved over the years. Another recently published book, *Circling Windrock Mountain* by Augusta Grove Bell, provides a vivid account of what the Coal Creek area was like a century or more ago.

As to the industrial development of Tennessee in the post Civil War period, it more or less reflects what had transpired in Pennsylvania a quarter of a century earlier. In a Ph.D. dissertation submitted to Yale University's Economics Department in 1900, Peter Roberts sets forth the economic conditions that led to the development of that state's coal mining industry (see his book, *The Anthracite Coal Industry*, which was published in 1901). By contrast, there doesn't appear to be any comparable indepth study of how either the coal or the iron/steel industry evolved in Tennessee itself. Even on turning to the *Encyclopaedia of Appalachia* one finds that Tennessee's coal industry is almost entirely excluded at the expense of Pennsylvania.

Chapter 1: The Earlier Welsh Presence

Despite having left Wales at the relatively young age of sixteen, Evan Shelby has not been completely forgotten in his native land, a page or two having been devoted to him in D C Rees's book on Tregaron: *Historical & Antiquarian* (published locally in 1936). Almost a century earlier a biographical sketch had appeared in the American-published *Cyfaill*, 4, 353 (1841). Further elaboration on many of his accomplishments are to be found in Samuel C Williams's article, 'Shelby's Fort' found in *East Tennessee Historical Quarterly*, 7, 28 (1935). Under the heading 'Chickamauga Fight of 1779', his connection to Sale Creek was outlined by the *New York Times* in 1929, the 150th anniversary of the mentioned battle. Having been active in the affairs of Virginia for most of his life, it must have surprised even him in 1779 when, as a result of the boundary survey conducted by Walker Henderson, he found that he was a resident of North Carolina, after all. This accounts for why a biographical sketch by Paul W Beasley appears in the *Dictionary of North Carolina Biography* edited by William S Powell. Given his exploits at the frontier, it is only fitting that his eventual place of rest would be deemed to be in Tennessee. As to General Richard Winn, an account of his deeds can be found in the *Tennessee Historical Quarterly*, 1, 8 (1942) and a biographical sketch by Harry M Ward appears in *American National Biography*.

The Tredyfferin Baptist Church in the Philadelphia area was first organized around 1710 and, prior to the Revolution, one of its earlier ministers had spent several months amongst Native Americans in what was to become Ohio. This served to inspire some later church members to set out for the Smoky Mountains in 1819 and once there they expected to interact with the Cherokees. In the *Memorial of Thomas Roberts* which was edited by H F Smith and published in 1867, Thomas Roberts himself recalls some of the hazards they encountered while making their way through eastern Tennessee. A fascinating account of how their relationship with the Cherokees evolved can be found in the book *Champions of the Cherokees* (1990) by William G McLoughlin.

Of the many studies conducted on Samuel Roberts's lifelong commitment to aid his fellow countrymen, about the only one available to English readers is a book entitled *A Welsh Colonizer in Civil War Tennessee* which was published by the University of Tennessee Press in 1961. The author, Wilbur S Shepperson, also had another article 'A Welsh Settlement in Scott County, Tennessee' published in the *East Tennessee Historical Quarterly*, 18, 162 (1969). In his *Taith o Lanbynmair i Cincinnati* [A Journey from Llanbrynmair to Cincinnati] which was published in Cincinnati in 1857, Samuel Roberts provides an account of his journey up to that point. A chapter which deals with his time in Tennessee can be found in the book *Cofiant y Tri Brawd o Lanbrynmair* [Memoirs of the Three Brothers from Llanbrynmair] by E Pan Jones. This had been published in Wales in 1893 and a recently published article on his idealism by Daniel Williams, in a 2004 issue of *Taliesin*, is indicative of how he remains a figure of considerable interest and controversy in Wales.

As to the fate of soldiers who participated in the Civil War, numerous accounts were to appear in both *Y Drych* and the denominational magazines, including the Baptists's *Y Seren Orllewinol* [The Western Star] which was published out of Pottsville, Pennsylvania. One interesting account comes from a letter preserved by descendants of the soldier's family. As to the Confederates, details concerning the post-war plight of Mary Jones Polk Branch's family is taken from her book, *Memoirs of a Southern Woman*, which was published in 1912. With the Rev. D W Phillips, who founded the Nashville Normal and Theological Institute, an account of his struggles can be found in a bi-monthly magazine published out Cincinnati under the title *The Cambrian*, 2, 112 (1882).

Chapter 2: The Industrial Background

The flow of Welsh miners into Pennsylvania pre-dates many other nationalities and appears to have started around 1830. This is when one starts to hear of their presence in such places as Pottsville and Carbondale. By mid century an even greater number were to find their way into the state's principal mining area that extended from Wilkes-Barre to Scranton. A detailed survey of their presence here appeared in the two issues of *Y Drych* that bridged the years of 1867 and 1868.

As to the limited presence of the Welsh in pre Civil War Tennessee, their attempts at producing iron are alluded to in the series of articles published in the weekly newspaper *Colomen Columbia* [Columbian Dove] during 1892/3 and that went on to deal primarily with their post Civil War achievements. Though a more generalized accounting of such earlier attempts at producing iron can be found in Goodspeed's 1887 *History of Tennessee*, the details are rather limited. Other publications such as *Origin & Development of the Tennessee Coal, Iron and Railroad Company* provide additional details regarding the development of particular companies. This valuable account is based on a lecture given by a former president of the company, Robert Gregg, in 1948. More recently the site of another of Chattanooga's earlier furnaces became the subject of an archaeological investigation – see *Industry and technology in antebellum Tennessee: the archaeology of Bluff Furnace* (1992) by R Bruce Council, Nicholas Honerkkamp and M Elizabeth Will. For what transpired within the iron industry in the southern states during the war, refer to Anne Knowles's article 'Labor, Race, and Technology in the Confederate Iron Industry' in *Technology and Culture*, 42, 1 (2001).

The brief comment regarding the initial attempt at mining copper in Ducktown comes from the series of articles cited above in *Colomen Columbia* (December 1892). As to the ill-fated attempt at opening a slate quarry, the text reproduced in the appendix has been taken from R R Williams's account 'Ychydig o Atgofion am fy Arosiad yn Madisonville, Tennessee'

[A Few Memories of my Stay in Madisonville, Tennessee] which was published by *Y Cyfaill* [The Friend], 59 , 219 (1896).

Chapter 3: Opportunities after the War

In an article on 'Cymry yn Knoxville, Dwyreinbarth Tennessee' [The Welsh in Knoxville, Eastern Tennessee] which was published in *Y Cenhadwr Americanaidd* [The American Missionary], 32, 23 (1871), their first pastor, the Rev. Thomas Thomas, gives an insight as to what Knoxville was like on their arrival immediately after the war. Also included in his account are some of the details pertaining the to mill's ownership and operation. Though the details vary somewhat, esentially the same picture emerges from Goodspeed's 1887 *History of Tennessee*. A letter that refers to their early progress, and written by David Richards in conjunction with J H Jones, appeared as part of a longer article in the *New York Times* on 6 December 1868. Further information regarding the company's production capabilities appeared in J B Killbrew's 1880 report, 'Knoxville as an Iron Centre', as well as in an *Atlanta Constitution* article entitled 'Nails' (27 June 1882). An account of their different responsibilities within the company can be found in the series of articles that appeared in the weekly newspaper, *Colomen Columbia* [Columbian Dove] during the years of 1892/3.

As well as providing an insight as to how Mechanicsville came into being, the same series of articles go on to discuss the activities of those not directly involved in the iron industry. The Knoxville Furniture Company, which is also referred to in Goodspeed's history book, was one of three such furniture companies that provided employment for many in the city. Through being familiar with the handling of roofing slate, others would have a significant impact on the city's construction industry. Prior to the formation of a company that eventually came to be owned by R W Owens, there were only two houses in all of Knoxville that could boast of having a slate roof. According to *Colomen Columbia* [Columbian Dove] the one responsible for roofing those two initial buildings was a William O Thomas who had been "twice around the world". As inconsequential as such a passing remark appears to be, it proved sufficient to identify the individual concerned.

As a nine year-old in 1854 he had started working in the slate quarries of Ffestiniog. On reaching 20 his mother made the mistake of allowing him to accompany two friends as far as the port of Liverpool. Instead of returning home as she had instructed, he couldn't resist the temptation of joining them on a ship bound for New York. On arrival, and through the bard, Ionoron, he found work at one of the slate quarries in Vermont. Not content to stay there indefinately, he started to wander around the southern states until he finally found Nashville to his liking. One can only presume that it was during his three-year stay there that he had briefly worked in Knoxville. In 1874 the Tennessee Car Roofing Company appointed him to be their travelling agent in California and it was while there that he had undertaken the voyages which are chronicled in his book *Dwywaith o Amgylch y Byd* [Twice Around the World] and published in Utica, New York in 1882. It was only after such travels that his mother would see him again.

As informative as anything, when it comes to the early years of Coal Creek, are the previously referred to series of articles in *Colomen Columbia* and then Goodspeed's *History of Tennessee*. Providing the basis for what can be gleaned about the earlier years of Oliver Springs are Augusta Grove Bell's book, *Circling Windrock Mountain* (University of Tennessee Press, 1998) and then the Rev. Lot Lake's account of his visit (30 November 1882 issue of the weekly newspaper, *Y Drych*). As to Soddy, one of the more fascinating accounts is that given in an article entitled 'Underground: Down in a Tennessee Coal Mine' that appeared in the 18 June 1882 issue of *The Atlanta Constitution*. Apart from providing a factual account of the mining operation, the paper's correspondent managed to convey to his readership a sense of what it was like to work underground. Prior to his Oliver Springs visit, the Rev. Lot Lake had also been in Soddy, and his reflections on the place can be found in the *Drych* article cited above. Then, visiting Soddy around the same time was D I Jones, editor of an English-language bi-monthly magazine known as *The Cambrian*. Included in an article entitled 'A visit to Soddy and Chattanooga, Tennessee', 2, 112, (1882) are many informative observations on Chattanooga's iron industry. The degrading comments regarding the background of those who came from Aberdare have been taken from Benjamin Evans's *Bywgraffiad T. Price, Aberdâr* [Biography of T Price, Aberdare] (1891).

Once again it is the same series of articles from *Colomen Columbia* [Columbian Dove] that provide most of what was is known about the Welsh presence in the Jellico area. As to the Cardiff Coal and Iron Company, a promotional pamphlet released in conjunction with a stock offering in 1890 is the only known source of information regarding its existence. As to the so-called 'Antie Peggy' who ran the boarding house in Coal Creek, details regarding her have been taken from 'Memoir of Mrs Margaret Davies' – a copy of which has been preserved by the family. No indication is given as to where it was published and about all that can be said regarding it is that it was authored by I G (presumably Iorthyn Gwynedd) and, contrary to the custom at the time, its language is English.

Chapter 4: Conflicts and Disasters

The so-called Coal Creek War has been the subject of numerous studies and Augusta Grove Bell devotes a chapter to it in her book, *Circling Windrock Mountain*. The brief account given in the present work is based on contemporary accounts and in this respect, the 21 and 22 July 1891 issues of the *Washington Post* have been particularly useful. On 25 September 1887, the same paper had drawn attention to safety issues in mines worked by convicts. As to the plight of Coal Creek's Welsh, the *Knoxville Journal* would later recall in their 15 July 1891 issue, the comments of their editor who had been present at the arrival of the first convicts.

The dangers associated with coal mining in general are reflected by the frequency of the reports that appeared in *Y Drych* over the better part of the nineteenth century. While these deal primarily with accidents that occurred in Pennsylvania, the Tennessee mines also experienced horrific accidents. In his *Seventy Years in the Coal Mines* (1935), Philip Francis describes his own participation in the rescue attempt after a Coal Creek mine explosion. On 10 December 1911, the *New York Times* was to report on another major disaster in Briceville. Details regarding an isolated train explosion in Soddy have been taken from the 26 May 1886 issue of *The Atlanta Constitution*. Information regarding the status of black workers in an industrial environment can be found in the 1941 book *The Negro in Tennessee, 1865–1880* by A A Taylor of Fisk University. In the previously cited *Atlanta Constitution* article from 1882, attention is drawn to the way some African-Americans employed by the Knoxville Iron Company had progressed beyond performing the more menial tasks. For a discussion of the ballads related to mining, as well as examples of the ballads themselves, see George Korson's *Coal Dust on the Fiddle, Songs and Stories of the Bituminous Industry* (1965).

Chapter 5: Adhering to Welsh Traditions

Comments related to the formation of Knoxville's Welsh Society can be found in the 3 December 1891 issue of *Colomen Columbia*. The same paper carried a brief account of David Richard's address to the society in its 14 April 1892 issue. As to their post-eisteddfod farewell dinner to Gwilym Eryri, a summary of the evening's proceedings have been preserved through a newspaper cutting (possibly from the same newspaper) in the possession of one of the families. The account is headed 'Ffon a phen aur i Gwilym Eryri' [A Gold-Headed Cane for Gwilym Eryri].

Most of what is known about their church in Knoxville comes from what was written by two of its earliest ministers, Thomas Thomas and Iorthyn Gwynedd. When Thomas Thomas submitted his article to *Y*

Cenhadwr Americanaidd [The American Missionary] in January 1871, they had already committed $2,000 towards a new church building. As something in excess of $1,000 was still needed, it explains why the project didn't come to fruition until April 1873, and it was then that it was officially opened according to Iorthyn Gwynedd's article, 'Profedigaeth Chwerw Iorthyn Gwynedd' [Iorthyn Gwynedd's Bitter Experience], which appeared in the same magazine: 34, 298 (1873). In the article he dwells at some length on how Dr Joseph Levi, amongst other church members, had helped him overcome his enormous sense of grief through being away at the time of his wife's untimely death.

Details regarding some of the church-related activities can be found in both Goodspeed's *History of Tennessee* and the 29 December 1872 issue of the *Knoxville Daily Chronicle*. While bearing no ill-will towards the new church, a select few (possibly of Anglican background) decided not to join, but little exists regarding their eventual fate. Exceedingly helpful when it came to locating the headstones of many of the earlier families was 'Obituaries of Knoxville's Welsh', which had been compiled by Robert McGinnis (unpublished).

What is known about their church in Soddy is based to a large degree on what the Rev. Lot Lake wrote after his 1882 visit (see 30 November 1882 issue of *Y Drych*). As to the churches in the vicinity of Jellico, one has to rely almost exclusively on odd comments found in the series of articles that appeared in *Colomen Columbia* around the time when many of them were organized. The anticipated participation of Henry Clay in the Chatanooga Eisteddfod is mentioned in an article that discussed the ongoing arrangements for hosting the event (1 October 1891 issue of *Colomen Columbia*). As to Dr L Jones Price, and in addition to an article about him in the same paper, he seems to have been about the only person of Welsh extraction to have a biographical note included in *Goodspeed's History* (under Anderson County).

Listed in the Chattanooga Eisteddfod programme are some events not cited in the present discussion. These included competitions for brass bands, always popular with mining communities, and essays that ranged from the Welsh participation in the Revolution to what factors favoured the continued development of Chattanooga. While the stanzas to Lookout Mountain have been preserved through the pages of *Y Drych* (22 September 1892), the winning entry in the competition regarding General George Thomas is yet to surface. The account of the rebellious meeting regarding the use of convict labour comes from the 6 November issue of the *Chattanooga Times*.

Chapter 6: Industrial and Cultural Leadership

Several of the previously mentioned articles that were written for *Colomen Columbia* in 1892/3 are in the form of biographical notes on those who had risen to prominence within the coal and iron industry. In a yet to be published article on 'Networking among Welsh Industrial Immigrants', Ronald L Lewis of the University of West Virginia discusses some of the means of attracting workers to certain areas. Informative as well is his 2008 book, *Welsh Americans: A History of Assimilation in the Coalfields*.

As to Dr Joseph Parry's family relationship with many in the Knoxville area, some of the information has been taken from *Cofiant Dr Joseph Parry*, a biography of Joseph Parry by E Keri Lewis that dates from 1921. For a discussion of Iorthyn Gwynedd's contribution to the *Llyfrau Gleision* [Blue Books] see Gwawr Jones's article in *Y Cofiadur*, 62, 18 (1998). Some of the efforts to nullify the negative impact of the above report can be found in *Bywyd a Gwaith y diweddar Henry Richard* [The Life and Work of the late Henry Richard] by Eleazar Roberts (1907). The article on Knoxville that was written for the benefit of the children back in Wales appeared in the September 1873 issue of *Trysorfa y Plant* [Children's Treasury]. As to Rees and David Thomas whose books made it to Harvard's Widener Library, of enormous help have been the various cuttings preserved within the covers of a Welsh Bible that remains in the possession of the family.

Also from Y Lolfa:

PETER GRIFFITHS

Tongue

Tied

dinas

£9.95

ISBN: 978 1 84771 097 0

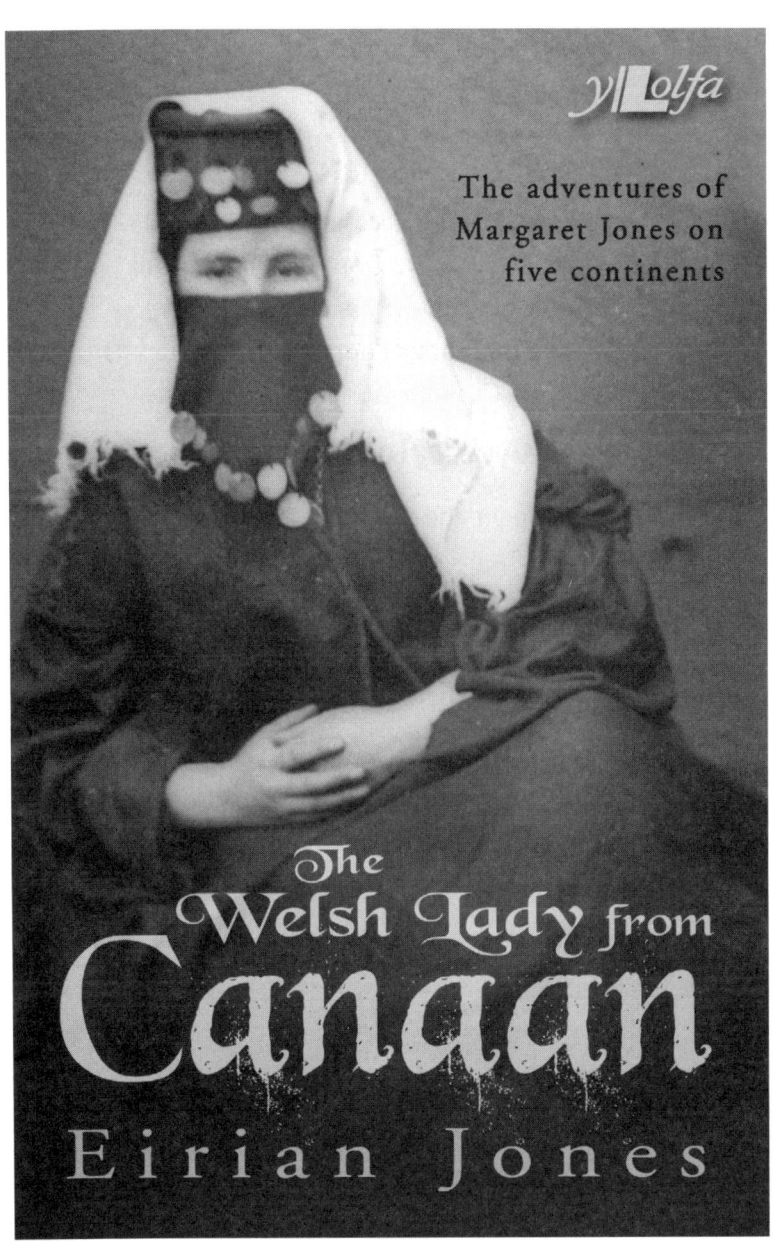

The adventures of
Margaret Jones on
five continents

The
Welsh Lady *from*
Canaan

E i r i a n   J o n e s

£9.95
ISBN: 978 1 84771 422 0